COULD QUESTIONS BE THE ANSWER?

DR. RANDY JOHNSON

Tellwell Talent
www.tellwell.ca

ISBN
978-0-2288-3877-7 (Hardcover)
978-0-2288-3876-0 (Paperback)
978-0-2288-3878-4 (eBook)

ENDORSEMENTS

As a psychologist and family therapist, I've read many books on communication in families and couples. Often these are aimed to teach family members or spouses skills: How to make yourself clear, how to speak about what you want without blaming others, how to listen and convey understanding, etc. Most of these skill-based books are mind-numbingly repetitive.

Dr. Randy Johnson takes a novel, and I would say, brilliant approach. Instead of trying to teach us how, he suggests we use questions as a foundation of effective communication. In so doing, he activates curiosity as a way to help couples and family members to communicate better and invite more helpful communication from their loved ones. The *title* is even a question.

Randy has structured this book in bite-sized chunks, with practical realistic examples – you will see yourself in many of them. The first five chapters lay the foundation – questions, not answers, as a way to improve communication. The middle of the book (Chapters 6, 7, and 8) gives the reader some jargon-free scientific and psychological information. Randy brings it home in the last five chapters with some specific guidance and suggestions for skills development and practice.

Could Questions be the Answer? That's something you will have to answer for yourself. Read this book with a questioning mind – *What can I learn? How can I better communicate and care for my loved ones?* and it's likely this book will help!

> Dr. Jeff Chang
> Registered Psychologist
> Associate Professor, Athabasca University

I have known Randy Johnson for many years now (around 36, I believe). We have been partners in many endeavours during that time. As I read Randy's manuscript, I came to appreciate a side of Randy I have not previously known. He has always been very insightful but Randy's book has further deepened my respect for his counselling and his Biblical and philosophical approach to life. His book is a practical guide on how to communicate well. I can think of a number of marriages that I am seeing that would benefit from the wisdom and communication expressed here

Randy has a plethora of wisdom on how to listen. That's why he continually refers the reader back to the importance of asking the right questions. As you work your way through this book, you will be convinced as I am, how vitally appropriate questions are. As Randy has pointed out, the timing and the type of question are essential for intimate dialogue and relationship to occur. Well timed and well-expressed questions are like a cold drink of water in a desert place. Randy has demonstrated this very well.

As a fellow psychologist, I have asked thousands of questions over my 40 years of counselling. But I must admit, Randy brings some new understanding to the value of questions and some fresh insights to me about how and where and why to ask astute questions. Randy's stories and illustrations do a great job of illuminating the valid points he makes throughout the book. He is able to help couples in counselling to communicate at a much deeper level. This book has potential to assist many marriages in their communication accuracy.

Although I discovered many helpful and practical insights in this book, I was especially interested in Randy's discussion in Chapter 11 on process and outcome. This is a helpful way of examining the reason that many couples do not communicate well or get caught in the trap of an all or nothing approach to communication. Also, Randy's discussion on forgiveness in Chapter 12 was particularly poignant for me in dealing with conflict crises. It has been my experience over many years that forgiveness is a major key for resolving relationship conflict and resolution.

I have one final question for Randy (lol). Who or what gave you the insight to ask so many good questions?! Well done, Randy. An excellent book.

Graham Bretherick
Registered Psychologist

Dr. Johnson has written a thoroughly readable and practical book to help us all create deeper and more meaningful relationships through the use of effective communication. He infuses each page with humor and examples taken from his career as a therapist to help us use questions to bridge gaps of misunderstanding and create productive dialogue. In this book we learn why we tend to fall into certain communication patterns, to identify our own blind spots and what we can do instead. He bases this information on neuroscience while also making it accessible for all. The scripts at the end of the book are especially helpful for showing how these techniques might look in real life, and for giving us hope. I expect I will be referring to this book in my work with couples in the future.

Corinne Mandin
Registered Psychologist

For those involved in role of persuading others, you need to know how to listen and effectively communicate. For many, the tendency is to engage in the role of facilitating change with passion and good intensions irrespective of the potential outcomes – good or bad. *Could Questions be the Answer?* invites the reader to consider the importance of being purposeful and intentional in how one uses words and the art of questioning to bring clarity to the evolving narrative in others. Dr. Johnson brings to light the art of asking questions with the intent to explore, understand and transform with a broad range of effective strategies underpinned by science and the wisdom gleaned from his many years as a therapist.

Dr. Wayne Hammond
Partner and Chief Science Officer
Flourishing Life

In a world where we frequently seem unable to hear one another, Dr. Johnson gives us the tools to hear and be heard. The answer is remarkably simple yet very effective: ask questions! A must-read for anyone that does not feel heard or has been accused of not listening – perhaps that is all of us.

Julie Lidstone MSW
Registered Social Worker

I love it when someone has a heart to get to the heart of things. As a performance capacity coach & trainer, I've witnessed that is where real change happens. That is the power of this book. I have known Randy for close to 20 years. Over that time, I have been privileged to witness the life changing impact he has had on so many in our community. He is the real deal with a genuine heart to get to the heart of things and make a difference. My definition of brilliant is the complex made simple. This book provides practical, insightful and realistic strategies around how the use of questions can be the key to better any relationship, whether at home or at work. Randy does so in a succinct, to the point manner, accented beautifully with a sprinkling of stories that will make you laugh, cry, and think. It is a book that is easy to read but will allow you to readily lift the concepts off the page and see them applied in your own life. It can help bring any relationship to some clear choices that can be made to see things improve. I'd recommend this book to both those people looking to work on improving personal relationships and leaders in organizations looking to facilitate effective teams that are engaged and motivated. This book can be a foundational pillar for your future success.

David Benjatschek
Building Performance Capacity Leadership Coach

ACKNOWLEDGEMENTS

I am extremely grateful to my wife, Cheryl, for her patience and persistence in providing significant editorial assistance on many long days, evenings, and weekends in the preparation of this book. Further, I am appreciative for her input into my life and how she has encouraged and supported me in so many of my adventures throughout our marriage. Thank you!

I am thankful to my family and friends who proofread the manuscript and provided invaluable feedback. The time you invested is much appreciated.

Thank you to my father-in-law for creating and designing the book cover.

Lastly, I thank my peers who read and endorsed this book. Your comments are very encouraging.

Table of Contents

Chapter 1

Communication – Not as easy as it sounds

"The proactive approach to a mistake
is to acknowledge it instantly,
correct and learn from it."
– Stephen Covey

Czech mate: Learning from our mistakes!

Several years ago, a colleague made a presentation at a leadership summit in the Czech Republic. Communication was already strained with the use of novice English interpreters who would relay the information from the presenter to the conference delegates, sentence by sentence, through the duration of the seminars and keynote presentations. To further complicate matters, my colleague, a Welshman, pronounced the letter "R" more like "Awe" than "Arrrrrrrrrrr."

In his presentation, he was emphasizing the importance of personal integrity and moral purity as a key character trait of exemplary leadership, with the exhortation to "guard your heart." However, with his R-dropping accent, it sounded like "God! Yaw' hot!"

The translator looked at the English-speaking guests in attendance, both from the UK and those from Canada, desperately searching for any possible help with this awkward translation moment. The UKers were of no help at all, only yelling the phrase "God! Yaw' hot!" with a similar accent as the presenter. The Canadians were of no assistance either because they were laughing too hard to say anything. My colleague tried to help by repeating the line with increased volume and frequency:

> "God, Yaw' HOT! GOD, Yaw' HOT! GOD
> YAW' HOT! GOD. YAW'. HOT."

He even added hand gestures, in the belief that people hear and understand you better when you use your hands.

The translator appeared confused, thinking, "What is this man saying?" It wasn't making sense. "Why was the presenter so insistent on flirting with the crowd?" The phrase begged for an interpretation.

Finally, one of the Canadians gained enough composure to venture out with a brief three-word clarification. Stifling his laughter, he gained the attention of the translator and emphatically clarified: "Guarrrrrrd yourrr hearrrrrrrt."

At last, the interpreter understood. With the clear rolling of the letter R, these three confusing words transformed into attainable understanding for him and for the entire audience. It only took seconds for the interpreter to ingest the words, process them and repeat them in fluid, concise and accurate Czech. It was actually very simple what the presenter was trying to say: "Protect your values. Keep safe your integrity." His words now made sense. He was proposing that good leaders lead organizations, teams and employees by using values, as opposed to telling those in attendance that, by the name of the Almighty, he found them sexually attractive.

Clearer communication, or breakdown?

It is amazing how a brief and clear enunciation of one little letter moved the entire presentation from a place of misunderstanding to comprehension. One missing letter changed everything! It does not have to be about a foreign language literally being misinterpreted. Confusion in communication happens to everyone from time to time, no matter the situation in which you find yourself.

There are two simple words in the English language that indicate being in a precarious position, a vulnerable place, past an important boundary: "Communication breakdown." These two words can signify the end of a negotiation, the dissolution of the business, the start of a strike, the end of a marriage, or the commencement of international conflict.

Historically, these two sobering words and their derivatives have been at the core of many sensational newspaper headlines. When communication breaks down, circumstances can get "messy" very quickly. We say things we wish we hadn't said, or say it in a way we didn't want to say it. Or perhaps what we said was misunderstood. Communication can easily get confused.

Conversely, when we hear the opposite of communication breakdown, such as "negotiations are still going strong" or "communication is healthy" or "at least they're talking again," there is a glimmer of hope. With good communication, even if our thoughts are at polarized positions, resolution is possible. Professional marriage therapists and psychologists say that the goal of counselling is not to avoid conflict, but to learn to fight fairly and to communicate effectively! People seek counselling for many reasons: not just to stop fighting, but primarily to learn and practice communicating more effectively.

Making a big deal of communication!

With all the tension and dramatic outcome surrounding misinterpretation, it is no wonder that public speaking is among the highest personal fears of people around the globe. This is because there is not only an increase of public scrutiny and a higher pressure to perform, but also a heightened potential for widespread miscommunication.

In reality, communication is rarely crystal clear. There is a lot of room for error. Communication mistakes are possible and common, even in writing. The smallest little comma can change everything. For example, "Enjoy your Thanksgiving turkey!" is a lovely comment to make just prior to the autumn harvest celebration. However, if the comma is re-positioned, the comment becomes mean-spirited - "Enjoy your Thanksgiving, turkey!" Because the potential for communication mistakes is high, asking questions that help bring clarification to the communicator's intention(s) can move a conversation quickly past a faux pas.

Frustrations in communication

Many things can go wrong when we try to communicate. This can cause frustration. Some sources of frustration include misinterpretation of facts, unclear expectations, differing perceptions, inaccuracy of words or meanings, distractions, and emotions. A story might be missing facts, or we might feel the embarrassment of being put on the spot in a meeting with unclear expectations. There can also be regret over a discussion in which we were expected to know what was being communicated, and we didn't. To make matters worse, we can beat ourselves up when we see that everyone else gets it, but we don't. The spontaneity of conversation can take us down an unpredictable road we did not want to venture on. Further, if someone is insecure, then bragging, defensiveness, exaggeration, or even lying might come into play.

Inattentive listening is a common source of frustration. Whether you are the speaker or the listener, you may need help navigating the conversation. Some people talk at such a rapid pace that a normal listener finds it difficult to follow their detailed narrative. Often such listeners become overwhelmed because they only want the basic facts. This is especially true with men. For example, a wife launches into recounting the events of her day, weaving a detailed narrative, sharing her feelings. The husband appears to be listening, but in actuality, is wondering if he needs to put gas in the car, or when the next hockey game is on TV. He may get this response: "Are you even listening to me?"

Then there's the couple not making any progress, increasingly frustrated with each other. Feeling that they need to unload their angst, one spouse takes the opportunity to divulge first, and goes off on their partner about not being present. The partner doesn't get it. They tune out. There isn't any worthwhile dialogue. They are both overwhelmed with emotion. It is as though they have had this same discussion a dozen times before, but still have gone nowhere.

Another example is the high school student who sits in class trying hopelessly to understand what the biology teacher is uninterestingly unpacking about photosynthesis. The student gazes despondently into the corner, wondering how this lesson will help them get a summer job. Just then the teacher calls on them for input and the 15-year-old can only offer back that deer-in-the-headlights look. They did not pick up what the teacher laid down. As the teacher explains it a second time, it only makes matters worse creating more anxiety and embarrassment.

Miscommunication causes shy people to become shyer. Timid people become unwilling to risk sharing much of themselves. Those who feel they are risking miscommunication, especially those unable to share feelings and emotions, become unable to convey more than mere facts. When couples stop communicating, they potentially drive back into their respective "caves of silence" because of the fear of blundering through feeble efforts to communicate. Every relationship experiences these common fears.

I admit there were times I have said the wrong thing, or I have said the right thing but in the wrong way. There have been times I have wanted to make a point, but my miscommunication just made things worse. While trying to resolve the issue, I unintentionally increased frustration.

There is an old adage from George Wilhelm Friedrich Hegel, a 19th century German philosopher that states: "We learn from history that we do not learn from history." I have met with hundreds of couples who have found themselves in the middle of the exact same argument yet again. It may be a different day, a different season, or even a different reason for the conflict, but the words are almost identical. There is no solution to the problem. Sadly, some people have been having the same arguments literally for decades. There is a cycle of repeated negative feelings with no resolution, when partners repeat contrary communication cycles, and both end up frustrated. History seems doomed to repeat itself, so they come to counselling looking for help.

Is there a way to fix miscommunication? Or are you too afraid to express your thoughts because so much damage has been done with words in past conversations?

There are probably times when your communication is adequate - no one is angry, things go well, the relationship is all wonderful and pleasant. Then the wheels fall off - maybe for a day, a week, or even more - and communication becomes a disaster, igniting powder kegs of emotional volatility. Maybe there are people you have been avoiding. Perhaps communication has broken down all together. If there is a recurring problem, conflict or "wall" that we hit, the wall may not be the problem. Maybe you could be partly to blame! Trying something new, learning something interesting, or changing something about how you communicate would be beneficial.

Is there a solution to miscommunication?

Breaking through a miscommunication barrier is first of all, about pathways to engagement. How can we initiate courteous, trust building dialogue? Could questions help us out? Could they help us find a way out of these conflicts and nightmare scenarios?

Caring questions come from thoughtful people who want to engage. Perhaps asking, instead of telling, could lead to a discovery of those seemingly distant and elusive relationship answers.

Chapter 2

Communication methods: Historically speaking

> "We thought that we had the answers,
> it was the questions we had wrong."
> – U2

I always feel bad for the guy at the microphone. I feel especially bad for the non-professional public speaker, the guy who did not attend Toastmasters but who is now making a toast. He is the guy who is first to grab the microphone before anyone else. Trying to be brave, he musters his confidence and crafts his words. Following his notes, he tries to look spontaneous and cool, like he has it all together. He starts talking, but no one can hear him. You see his lips move, the soundman hits the power button, and you hear those distressingly awkward words come bellowing out of the public address system: "IS THIS THING ON?" Communication was zero and now it is 100%. We heard nothing, and suddenly we hear everything.

What does truly effective communication look like? How do we know that we are being heard loud and clear? Does louder make it better? Are we actually being understood? How do we make that jump in real life, from zero to 100, powered up and belting it out?

Socratic method: Exploring contradictions

Socrates, one of the fathers of philosophy, lived in ancient Athens, Greece, from 469–399 BC. He was known for his work in ethics as well as philosophy, but lent his name to both Socratic Irony and the Socratic Method, his two most enduring legacies. Although 3,000 years old, the Socratic Method, known also in ancient Greek as "Elenchus," is engrained in today's philosophy and law. This method consists of asking repeated questions until a flaw or a contradiction is found in responses. Those asking questions can eventually find truth by process of elimination, which lets them discover the faulty hypothesis and remove that line of thinking. The high level of scrutiny through asking questions is the relentless tactic of the Socratic method: to move closer to what is accurate and pure. Through induction and definition, Aristotle, who gave credit to Socrates, took the Socratic method further by formulating the scientific method of reasoning.

This basis of ascertaining pragmatic logic through questions was one of Socrates' greatest contributions to humanity. In the fifth century BC, the contemporary Sophists mostly relied upon rhetoric, a powerful communication style using oratory with convincing eloquence to sway listeners. The most powerful communicator would win the day — even when wrong.

Socrates was a revolutionary thinker, who would deconstruct imperfect but persuasive thinking with simple questions. Like all good teachers, Socrates may have known most of the answers to his many questions. Often in a non-adversarial fashion, he disarmed those of a different school of thought by engaging them in another way of thinking. This method was the art and wisdom of Socrates. He profoundly changed the world with this new understanding.

King Solomon's method: Get understanding

Equally significant, ancient Hebrew writings employed a magnificent collection of proverbs written in a prose style. King Solomon, a brilliant man and revered leader, authored many of the proverbs found in Hebrew scriptures. His writing clearly differentiates between knowledge (knowing facts), wisdom (knowing how to process and proceed in light of those facts), and understanding (an accumulation of wisdom that led to higher, purer thinking and a transformed lifestyle). Solomon repeatedly encouraged his readers to "get understanding."

We should therefore assume that inquiry – or asking questions – gains understanding. For example, how does a child develop understanding? In the early years of development, children tend to ask lots of questions. They might ask, "Why is the sun in the sky?" or, "Why is the sky blue?" "Why? Why? Why?" If children do not ask questions, they will not learn, and they will not know for themselves. A two-year-old looking through a picture book does not say "apple, apple, apple, the round red mass with a stem on top...I've got to remember that." However, a toddler may pick up a yellow or green fruit and ask, "apple?" even though he knows it is not an apple. Mom responds, "No, that's a pear. Can you say pear?" Even with few reminders, he'll remember "pear" for life.

Developmentally, if a child is not asking questions, it is usually indicative of a problem. We evaluate parts of childhood development based on the questions children ask. Similarly, if a married couple does not ask each other, "How was your day?" we would assume that something is wrong – that the relationship must be having difficulties because there seems to be a lack of interest in one or both individuals towards their partner. Wanting to understand each other demonstrates love and appreciation.

Educational method: Encouraging development

Questions are essential to higher capacities of learning, especially learning beyond rote memorization. Broadly accepted education theory acknowledges that the most rudimentary form of learning is simply "to remember." If a child or a student can remember something, that does not necessarily mean they understand the idea. Little Johnny may know that the combined letters "g-r-a-s-s" spells "grass" and that grass is green. But at age five, he knows nothing about how chlorophyll blends with carbon dioxide, water, and sunlight to produce that green color and release oxygen for us to breathe. He does not yet understand photosynthesis.

Understanding is explored and captured well with questions like "Can you explain that?" "What is the meaning of that?" or "Can you summarize the process?"

Beyond fundamental remembering and understanding concepts, students acquire complex thinking with application, analysis, reflection, and creating. Again, questions provoke higher levels of learning.

A two-year-old remembers that the sky is blue, but not until his bedtime extends beyond daylight hours does he understand that the sun makes the sky blue, and that a sky becomes black at night when the sun is gone. At age four or five his analytical mind asks, "Why is the sky blue?" He might hear the simple response about refracted light in the earth's atmosphere from the blue spectrum, but he will not understand the color spectrum until age eight or nine when he does the classroom experiment with a glass prism and a light bulb in a darkened room and sees firsthand how rainbows are made. He analyzes and applies the facts from the prism illustration to the earlier question about blue skies. Then the lights come on for him. The inquisitive nature of the four-year-old wondering about the sky being blue finally makes sense. The attained knowledge will not be forgotten because self-learning (finding the answers to our own questions) leaves him with a feeling of fulfillment. That nagging question remaining from the heart of a four-year-old is finally solved.

When a textbook answers questions that no one is asking, the book remains on a shelf, dusty and unused. When we view the textbook as providing thousands of answers to meaningful questions, it takes on a whole new purpose, especially when the questions are important to the reader. Questions are the driving force behind the most retainable knowledge that students can engage with — knowledge they actually want. Great teachers lead students to ask great questions. Good parents draw their young children into discussion and present uncertainty that provokes them to ask questions. It is fine for Mom and Dad to be the encyclopedia of everything when kids are very young; we delight in being all-knowing for that season. However, it is not so fine when a 23-year-old calls home wanting to know what socks to wear, or even worse, why their sneakers smell funny because they have not been wearing socks at all!

Independent adult thinking requires analytical, applicable, evaluative, creative thinking, and problem solving. By the teen years, problem-solving skills are hopefully engrained with the gratifying repartee of frequent dialogue that includes asking questions and seeking answers. A common practice among teens during adolescent years is to answer "Why" when parents give them a directive. While many parents find this response from teens distressing, kids who show more maturity are prone to push back within reason when parents instruct them. It's part of maturation. They are becoming adults. It is annoying, certainly, but productive. It is exactly where our emerging students should be heading, down the recurring path of inquiry, remembering, and understanding – but ultimately heading towards higher levels of thinking. Growing children will not continue doing everything we say. We want more for them, to see them analyzing, applying, evaluating, and creating as they learn to question the adult way.

Counselling method: Active listening

To improve communication, we can embrace a choice of methods; the previously mentioned Socratic Method, Solomon's method, or an educational method. All three provide helpful insight.

Have you ever been deeply engaged in conversation with someone, but fully lost the moment when the phone rang? Has an incoming text message pulled away your attention? Even worse, you remain undistracted, but manage to not hear, or even totally miss, what your spouse, boss, coworker, or friend said? We call that "passive" listening. Your ears may have registered the sounds and your mind processed the words as intelligible and distinguishable English words, but it barely impacted you.

Full participation in conversation requires patience and perseverance – not only to say what is right, but also to carefully listen, actively participate, and truly hear, and clearly understand what is being said. Whether a professional counselling situation, a business meeting, a job interview, or simply paying attention to your neighbor describing his weekend adventure, each requires careful, active listening. I practice the techniques of active listening daily in my professional life, my relationships, my work teams, or any context that benefits from better communication.

For those not familiar with active listening, let me offer a quick overview. Active listening is a core skill from the skill set of counsellors, psychologists, social workers, and others in the "helping" profession. The following insights provide a great resource for individuals wanting to carefully listen and understand others. It includes the following skills:

- <u>Mirroring:</u> Do not just listen. Repeat back what has been said so you are sure you understood clearly. "Did I understand you to say…"
- <u>Summarizing:</u> Repeat back the major points you just heard. "So, I think you just said these four points…"
- <u>Agreement:</u> Offer back prompts that show you are listening. "Uh-huh… yeah…and then what happened next?" These comments are doubly effective when accompanied by nodding.
- <u>Interactive Feedback:</u> Share your responses and evaluations. "Was that shocking for you when that happened?" "I don't think that seems fair…"
- <u>Emotional Reflection:</u> Help them communicate with you by putting feeling labels on what they are saying. "Did that make you feel happy? Energized? Fulfilled? It sounds like maybe that was offensive, hurtful, or bothersome to you? Did that anger you?"
- <u>Affirmation:</u> Let the one communicating feel safe and validated in sharing their heart. "Thanks for sharing that with me. That was courageous of you to discuss that openly."
- <u>Non-comparative Comments:</u> Rather than rushing into your story by way of contrast or comparison, just keep listening and asking more questions. "Wow. Tell me more. Is there anything else about this?"
- <u>No Pat Answers:</u> Your friends and family are not looking for a brush off or "quick fix" answer.

Avoid saying, "It'll be alright, it's all gonna work out, why stress? Don't worry." Cliché answers will not help.

- <u>Non-interruptive Dialogue:</u> Your long pause tells the other person that you are interested, caring, and willing to hear more.

- <u>Non-Verbal Listening Techniques:</u>

  - Turn off, silence, or put away your phone.
  - Turn off the TV and minimize other background noise or distraction.
  - Literally lean towards the one who is talking.
  - Make eye contact.
  - Let your face mirror what the person is saying (disgust, joy, disappointment).
  - Nod in agreement when appropriate.
  - Appropriate touching with family or dear friends can be thoughtful. For example, taking and holding their hand, patting, or holding the forearm, or shoulder shows tenderness for someone who is upset.

Once you have actively listened, you will hear "highlighted" words or phrases that can be very significant to the conversation. Such words are emphasized, repeated, or they just stand out. When your friends and family members feel safe in talking to you because you genuinely listen and care, it is astounding what will come up to the surface – whether they are trying to share deep thoughts and ideas, or not. As you dig into the highlighted words, communication moves from shallow, passive interaction to deeper, more meaningful discussion.

I recall a group phone conversation where the opening "small talk" generated by participants was, "How was your week?" After a few casual comments, one member asked, "How about you, Paul? What's up?"

Fortunately for Paul, or perhaps unfortunately for Paul, this weekly phone group was comprised of several professionals learning coaching techniques and brushing up on their listening skills. Paul offered a short synopsis of his weekend – gardening, lawn maintenance, and some unfinished yardwork he had brushed off and was content to leave in what he called the "procrastination column." But it was the brief comment that followed the word "procrastination" that caused group members to take exception. Paul casually tacked on "procrastination...you know...the story of my life."

"Really?" someone asked who actively listened. "*That's your life story?*" That phrase was highlighted to the active listener as it seemed odd and out of place for Paul to make a life-assessment based on an unfinished task in a superficial discussion about the weekend.

"Uh-oh," said Paul, "I'm outed!" For the next 20 minutes, Paul became the object of care, discussion, accountability, and a veritable coaching clinic as his peers called him out on his words. They made him take responsibility for his words and actions. His negativity and procrastination, which he had tolerated as a part of his supposed "unchangeable" lifestyle, were quickly resolved. The group listened carefully enough to make a difference.

Communication interferences

Contrast is a powerful teacher. It not only tells us "what it is," but it also shows us "what it isn't." It is good to know about effective communication, but it is also good to know what can interfere with the process. I believe it will help us at this point to address filters and a list of "Communication No No's."

Filters

"Filters" refer to pre-conceived concepts, ideas, judgments, stereotypes, emotions, contexts, or moods that alter communication. The filters we use in daily life dynamically impact our communication. They change every conversation and transform what is said and heard. We all may hear the exact same words spoken, but each person involved in the discussion may use differing filters and varying interpretations. Parts of the discussion are heard differently by various cultures represented in the dialogue. Males and females reflect uniquely;

varied families of origin and backgrounds cause us to process differently; all of the various personalities and styles represented bring unique perspectives. When information becomes public, every component serves as a distinct filter, both in speaking and in how people understand the conversation. The many perspectives from the endless filters cause understanding to vary.

Even though good summary questions at the end of a conversation help establish takeaways, action plans, and next steps, the filters can still cause damage as they bring confusion and uncertainty. What filters did you bring into your relationships? What filters do others bring?

With good pre-marital counselling and early marriage follow-up and/or marriage mentors, a husband and wife *can* start the process of identifying pre-existing filters quickly in their relationship. As they work to understand each other, they create new filters to understand their marriage. The older filters get replaced.

Look at Miles and Janice. Miles has a filter of "poor me" from his childhood upbringing and first marriage. Janice has a filter of anger with Miles because he is more focused on his sons than on his new wife. The angrier Janice gets with Miles, the sorrier Miles feels for himself because all he is trying to do is help his boys recover from the divorce; his sons need this extra attention. Miles and Janice now have a goal to understand their respective old filters. Ideally, they will establish new filters to minimize the intensity of conflict, therefore reducing the damage they can cause in this new relationship.

Communication No No's

Poor communication or no communication is the greatest source of marriage breakdown that I see in clients who come for help. A lack of great communication kills relationships, especially marriages. Miscommunication leaves both spouses reeling – feeling unloved or neglected. Once identified, many communication issues have clear and simple solutions. Let me point out 16 such issues:

1. Mindreading

You might think you know what other people are thinking. You may know what they have thought historically. You might even know what they were thinking two hours earlier. The truth is, you do not know what other people are thinking. Attempting to read someone's mind will only cause problems in relationships.

I have seen many clients worry about a situation that is not even real; it is all in their mind. They thought they could read their partner's mind. Rather than reaching unwarranted conclusions, just ask your partner what they are thinking.

Ann thought her relationship with David might be over. She suspected he had lost interest in her. Although far-fetched, she wondered if he might even be having an affair. She thought he didn't care anymore. Ann was encouraged to ask David directly, and she did. He was not having an affair, he was still interested in her, and he was very much in love with her. However, he was facing a mountain of difficulty at work – that is all! Ann's fears and suspicions had driven a wedge between her and David. With open and direct communication, a simpler path emerged toward an improved marriage.

2. Dumping

Depending on our personality type, we all communicate differently. Some people process verbally while others prefer to sit and ruminate before they express their feelings. Timing is everything. If you have been holding on to negative emotions all day, you may feel like dumping all of those emotions on your spouse as soon as you get in the door. That would not be wise.

Those more passive in nature may want to share their feelings after having a significant time to process. Those strong feelings might also leak out in a moment of intense conversation. Some want to process feelings immediately while others need time. Either way, one should ask, "When can we talk about this? Later today? Tonight? Tomorrow sometime?" When we take time to process, we are more likely to have intelligent conversation that leads to a practical solution.

3. Interrupting

Do you find it irritating when someone tries to finish your sentence, or cuts you off to correct you, or because they think they know better? First of all, interrupting is rude. If we cannot treat our friends and, especially, our spouses with a higher level of respect, it reflects poorly on ourselves. We sometimes interrupt because we think we are "mind readers." In the Biblical book James 1:19, it advises us: "You must all be quick to listen, slow to speak, and slow to get angry." (New Living Translation)

When we actively listen to others, we listen carefully to every word they say. We wait until they are finished. We pause, then ask if they have anything more to share. To make sure we are clear, we repeat back to them a summary of their key points. Such techniques keep conversation calm and calculated, prevent conflict escalation, and leave the other person feeling that we hear and care.

Kevin and Leslie are both rational, professional, intelligent individuals. Their areas of disagreement were not huge. But when they sat together in my office, their blood boiled. They did not know how to fight fairly. They needed a referee more than a counsellor. When they stopped interrupting each other and learned how to listen, their marriage dynamic seemed to instantly change. All the misunderstandings self-corrected when they learned a simple skill. Their relationship moved into greater intimacy because they increased their courtesy towards each other.

4. Unsolicited Advice

Nobody likes a know-it-all. When we offer unsolicited advice, it can give an impression of arrogance, of knowing all the answers. Those who perpetually offer unsolicited advice may have a hard time keeping friends.

When people are talking, give them your full attention rather than focusing on solutions or your own ideas of how you can repair the situation. Instead, offer your support and affirmation. "I hear what you are saying. How did that make you feel? I imagine that must have been very difficult for you."

5. Criticizing

Criticism is another killer of relationships and communication. When a partner has the courage to authentically open up and genuinely share feelings and emotions, but the other partner dismisses them, deep hurt results. The tendency to be critical and fault-finding causes best friends to become fearful, skeptical, and untrusting especially when those who love them take advantage of their vulnerability.

To be certain, there will always be personal traits that annoy and irritate you in your closest relationships. Communicate openly and honestly, but do not be critical. You probably have heard of the power of "I" statements as opposed to "you" statements. Rather than accusing or criticizing, it is less threatening and less negative to share your needs prefaced with the words "I need…" In these cases, gentleness and humility go a long way in building effective communication, especially compared to accusatory and belittling statements.

6. Fuzziness

A lack of direct and clear statements, conclusions, or boundaries becomes a breeding ground for miscommunication. Once again, where personality types differ, there are many possibilities for miscommunication. When one partner in a marriage consistently is assertive or too aggressive and the other partner is too quiet or passive, misunderstanding is inevitable. Discussions, decisions, and dialogue all need clear boundaries and agreements to end entrenched discussions. Some couples write their points on paper and look them over with each other just to make sure everything they talked about was clear. It may be clear in your mind and it may be clear in your partner's mind, but you still may have differing points of view. Take away the fuzziness by recapping what you discussed and by mirroring each other's words.

7. "Have to Win" Mentality

Some couples do not realize their competitive behavior until the need to give the last word and winning the argument arises. When we discuss sensitive topics with our partners, there is an inherent win/lose tension. Our human nature loves to judge between right and wrong; as that old saying goes, "I can afford to be narrowminded because I am right!" Although funny, profound pain resides close to those we love when we adopt such a competitive attitude. Every winning situation necessitates that a "loser" be identified. Rather than ending a conversation with a clearly identified victor, conclude your conversation with words and thoughts of affirmation. Since most good marital communication ends in some form of compromise, celebrate what you love about each other rather than each partner having to concede a loss.

Tara, a frustrated stay-at-home mom, defused a heated conversation with her husband, Jack, in my office. Jack was doing a great job providing for home and family, but Tara was getting a little stir crazy being home with four kids. She was not feeling entitled or unappreciative, but she did need to vent about her fatigue, the crowded house, a lack of adult conversation, and how she missed her professional life. Jack worked long, hard hours to make ends meet. This mounting tension had him on the defensive until Tara softly offered these words, "I really appreciate how hard you work, Jack. I know you've made a lot of sacrifices for our family and for me." Jack's defensives melted and he responded, "I hear you, Tara." He proceeded to mirror back all her feelings in everything she said. The competition ended. They became teammates again instead of adversaries. Up to this point they had been competing to see whose life was harder and who had made greater sacrifices.

8. Autocratic Communication

Being bossy and treating others like children or subordinates is an easy way to drive people away and harm communication. No one likes taking orders from a spouse. We all function better when we dialogue and make decisions as partners instead of one person barking orders. We should draw circles instead of lines. Lines dictate ultimatums and directives; circles describe inclusivity, partnership, and shared hearts in every area of life. We need to move from "you" statements (accusatory), even beyond "I" statements (participatory), to "we" statements (inclusive) in our communication. The language of invitation and appeal develops healthy relationship communication.

9. Over-Promising, Under-Delivering

We lose credibility when we say "yes" too quickly or comply just to keep peace, even if it includes agreeing to diffuse or eliminate a conflict. This false compliance might work with people close to you, but will eventually cause frustration. You need to be truthful. If you tend towards being an enabler or a pleaser, understand that it is okay to say "no." It's healthier to have reasonable boundaries and it will save yourself from damaging burnout.

10. Blame shifting

Doug and Karen were on a never-ending treadmill of frustration. Doug always seemed to be on edge and angry about something, but never able to put a finger on it. Karen was sweet, gracious and forgiving, but to a fault. Doug was angry about how Karen spent money, but she was within reason, careful with the grocery money, and stayed within the family budget. Doug was upset about how Karen left too many lights on and kept the house overly warm. The resulting electricity and heating bills caused him a lot of frustration. He also complained that she was too extravagant with the kids, especially treats and outings. It became obvious that Doug's anger was about something deeper.

The real issue was revealed after many hours of discussion: eight years earlier, an unwanted pregnancy pushed them into "family status" sooner than they had planned. Even though they both had agreed during a written inventory exercise in their pre-marriage counselling that birth control was to be a shared responsibility, Doug blamed Karen for the pregnancy and shifted the "blame" to Karen for that "mistake." Nevertheless, Doug sincerely loved all his kids. He would not trade them for the world, but he repressed an underlying, illogical anger and blame towards Karen. Shifting the blame either in small or great situations can erode conversational and relational trust.

11. Narcissism

Narcissism is generally defined psychologically as a personality disorder in which an individual is too focused on themselves and their own ideas without listening to others. As you can imagine, narcissism can be powerfully destructive in communication.

Narcissism becomes exposed when clients perform their counselling homework assignments. Couples might agree on four steps for their homework; they wholeheartedly and mutually agree to the four steps, even recite those four steps back to me. When it comes time to follow up, one partner has not completed any of the four steps agreed upon but only did one small item mentioned weeks ago that had been discussed in passing. One partner had missed the pleas and desperate requests from the other partner. In such situations, it's best to put agreements in writing with dates; otherwise, a narcissistic spouse will remember only what he or she *wants* to remember.

12. Avoidance

Avoidance is a way to deflect conversation. Generally speaking, avoidance appears more prevalent in men.

When a conversation about an unwanted discussion or topic arises, some just shut it down. They avoid the topic or go silent in the most extreme cases. This phenomenon, known as "stonewalling," will be discussed later. Just because people are ill-equipped to handle their emotions or a high level of emotional discomfort, it's not an excuse for them to behave this way. While appropriate for a two-year-old, it's not acceptable in adults. Gentle confrontation is helpful. Questions such as, "Can you talk about which parts of this conversation are difficult for you?" or, "Can we break them down one by one?" or, "Can we talk about some of it today and some of it another day?" These questions can defuse a mountain of a problem into smaller, more manageable hills. This helps when tackling what might seem to be an overwhelming issue.

Stacey was totally unwilling to discuss intimacy issues in her marriage. This is understandable as she had been assaulted in her earlier years. In fact, a teenaged babysitter had spoken to her inappropriately when she was nine years old. The experience had violated her and, accordingly, she had never felt comfortable in intimate situations, not even with her husband. As a result, she was not prepared to talk about her marriage until the root issue had been exposed, discussed, and healed. Once the issue had been reviewed in manageable segments, Stacy stopped avoiding intimacy with her husband.

13. Assumption

When we falsely assume that others clearly understand what was said but don't use interactive dialogue, this leads to dysfunctional communication. People need an opportunity to ask "How?" or "Why?" or "What?" for clarity. Once again, mirroring conversation that repeats back what was said helps the listener. Unhurried open dialogue is one of our greatest resources and ensures clear communication.

Todd, a successful businessman, could not retain employees in the long term. Confident and self-directed, he knew what he wanted. He held brief staff meetings, provided distinct instructions to his employees, then directed them to work. Consequently, with little two-way dialogue, his employees were confused, highly frustrated, and therefore, they underperformed. Most resigned within a year.

14. Yelling

Yelling is a playground behavior and is not appropriate for adults. Aside from emergencies such as shouting "Fire!" or "Look out!" or "Help!" yelling is otherwise ill-mannered and unprofessional. When you raise your voice at your good friends, your family, colleagues, or even strangers, nothing will be accomplished. You may desire to be heard, but the louder you speak, the less people will actually "hear you."

Linus, of the famed *Charlie Brown* show, prevented a situation from escalating by quoting Solomon in Proverbs 15:1: "A soft answer turns away wrath." The Proverb offers great advice. When the situation around you grows louder, respond softly and you will calmly take the wind out of "anger's sails."

I remember countless times while counselling in my office when emotions spiraled out of control and tempers were on the verge of flaring. I would smile and gently suggest, "Let's just back away from this for a moment," and cooler heads would eventually prevail. By appealing to the best in people, they often respond with their best behaviors.

15. Timing

Even when we approach issues with all the grace in the world, sometimes it's just too early to address "that" issue. Our hurt or pain is often associated with the topic of discussion. Moreover, anger or rage may even develop. Avoidance of such issues is not acceptable. An action plan is required for when the issue can be discussed. A delay of a day, week, or even a month may be necessary. In the meantime, appropriate questions and dialogue will open discussions of smaller issues that will eventually connect to the bigger issues with disciplined follow-through over time.

Mr. Schultz was an older gentleman who had fought in World War II. He had seen and experienced unspeakable atrocities that caused him to struggle with post-traumatic stress disorder (PTSD). He had vowed never to burden his family with those stories, vowing to take his secrets to the grave. In the early 1980s, his marriage faced problems that arose from roots of anger and PTSD. Although tragic that he carried post-war pain for 40 years, both his wife and I were profoundly thankful that he finally came to terms with this pain. He remarked that he had not experienced happiness since he was a young boy. He never fully resolved the effects of PTSD, but eventually overcame enough that the final 10 years of his life were his happiest.

16. Complaining

Most believe that identifying the problem is only half the solution. While it's good to identify issues and problems, many people, especially couples, can spin their wheels for prolonged seasons at this first point of identification. Many get trapped in the cycle of complaining and will oppose clear, concrete action plans, and some people just like to complain. However, rather than allowing endless criticism, it's more helpful to identify the problem and move forward with specific, measurable, achievable, relevant, and time-sensitive objectives.

Edgar and Charlotte, an older couple reluctant to change, seemed content to sit in my office complaining week after week about each other and all of their faults. In a confrontational moment, I challenged their relentlessly negative attitudes. I suggested we map out a way forward. Oddly enough, the solutions were so easily found that I only saw the couple twice more.

Even as I review these 16 Communication No No's, I recognize that not one of them is entirely perfect. Our blunders in the heat of the moment can escalate disagreements. Changing how we communicate does not come easily, yet I believe that it is possible and attainable when we use understanding, practice, and patience.

Chapter 3

What questions bring to the conversation

Questions bring 10 fundamental components to a conversation:

- Clarity
- Direction and structure
- Reasonable doubt
- Empowerment
- Influence
- Invitation
- Fulfillment
- Affirmation
- Care and compassion
- Comforting confines
- Connection

Clarity

Journalist François Gautier said, "More important than the quest for certainty is the quest for clarity." It is all about clarity. The greatest tool we have in creating and maintaining healthy relationships is communication. When communication breaks down, relationships disintegrate. When communication is unclear or when there are misunderstandings, trouble presents itself. Even before understanding can exist, you have to be clear. Clarity comes first and foremost by understanding each other and through having healthy, functional relationships.

Whenever there is uncertainty, whenever clarity is lacking, there is no tool as effective as a simple question:

- What did you mean by that?
- What did you just say?
- Can you repeat that please?
- So, you are saying that...?
- Am I to understand that you're saying...?

Once things have been clarified, the person can process what has been said within their context. The listener can then relate and perhaps even move towards a position of understanding. Clarity puts people on the same page, or at least gets them reading from the same book. Sometimes it may feel you are in different libraries, but clarity helps bring you to the same place.

There has been a significant amount of writing on the subject of men and women being different. One such author is Dr. John Gray who titled his book *Men Are from Mars, Women Are from Venus* (1992) to point out how significantly different men and women are with respect to communicating. But before we write it all off as being sexist or stereotypical nonsense, perhaps we could learn from the natural gender difference in how we think. I suspect that getting some clarity in this regard would be tremendously beneficial to the relationship conflicts that daily darken the doors of my office.

According to Dr. Gray, when a woman shares information, it typically is more than just a few facts. From what I have seen for a female in the counselling setting, the test of taking the conversation to the next level lies in the clarity. I have found that when a woman asks, "Do you understand?" what she is really asking is, "Can I trust you with more? Do you perceive what I am saying and what I am feeling?" If this level of understanding occurs, a woman will give more information about what she wants. She will not often start out this way, but if she trusts, if she feels safe, she will share about what she really wants.

Men, by contrast, have more of a fix-it mentality. They do not tend to tune in to words – especially the feelings behind the words – as much as the actions they need to perform in order to repair the situation and get out of my office as quickly as possible.

Consequently, the script often goes like this:

- Wife: "You don't hear what I'm saying!" (She gets defensive.)
- Husband: "I heard you!" (He is also getting defensive.)
- Wife: "No, you didn't." (Thinks to herself, "I don't trust him to really understand who I am. He just wants to fix me. I just came to share. I just want to feel connected to him.")
- Husband: "Sure I do honey!"

The issue with the husband is simple. He assumes one thing – "She needs help!" – and it is the wrong thing. He probably sees her as a damsel in distress. He is in the wrong game entirely. He has shown up, but he is at the wrong field, with ice skates on his feet, a baseball bat in his hand, and a basketball jersey on his back.

How can I, as a therapist, offer any help to suggest that they need parameters, the kind of boundaries that questions provide? How can I help him focus as I initiate the conversation? Often, I share something like this: "I need you to listen as I share this simple concept. Do you remember moments ago I asked you to listen, not to fix it? Do you recall we had an agreement at the outset of our appointment? Did we not agree that your wife would get the emotional support she wants and needs? Did we not mutually agree that you would *not* do anything, that you only have to listen?"

The husband might be frustrated. But he has to listen. He has to get it done. Otherwise, the couple will remain at odds and continue to trigger each other's needs. For her, the need is this: "I need you to listen." For him, the need is this: "I need to fix it." That variance of needs is a recipe for disaster. He can fix it only by listening intently. It may be like mental gymnastics for him; he needs these simple boundaries of "just listening." Period. He has to say to himself, "If she really wants me to fix her or if she wants to know what I think, then she *has to* actually ask me out loud for that. Otherwise, I will remain quiet, and not try to fix the situation." If he understands that, then he can stay focused.

This is how husbands can create an environment of care and compassion for their wives. The same strategies utilized in marital relationships apply to all relationships. Ultimately, people need to know they are listened to and cared for. President Theodore Roosevelt seemed to articulate it best: "People don't care how much you know until they know how much you care."

People need to feel a measure of security in conversation. When you care about how people think or feel, they will not be as defensive. Those reared in environments of abuse or conflict, have a greater need to be heard and shown care.

Beth was a victim of assault by an alcoholic, abusive father. Stephen was a loving and gentle husband to her. Yet when they experienced conflict, Stephen was not much help to his hurting wife. His significant breakthrough came when we talked through the simple boundary of being quiet while listening carefully to his wife – only asking questions when appropriate. Rather than trying to "be right" or "win" the argument, he needed to back off and take leadership in the relationship; this demonstrated loving leadership, not controlling leadership. Asking questions became Stephen's platform for successful discussions with Beth. He began to listen intently, then ask her clarifying questions to break down the walls, one at a time. She was not angry with him. When he stopped trying to "fix her" and instead listened intently, he could finally *hear* what she was saying. In many regards, she was still a terrified 10-year-old girl – her age when she started being abused. She was very fearful. The more Stephen and I listened and asked questions, the more apparent it became to Beth that Stephen was not the cause of her problems at all. By not listening and always trying to fix her, he had made matters worse. He learned to relax, not to try and fix Beth. She began to trust him more because he *really* wanted to hear. The more he listened, the more he asked, and trust was increasingly built. Subsequently, they began to feel more comfortable with each other. Her need was huge, and Stephen's questions showed that he truly cared. They ascended in an upward vortex of hope rather than a downward spiral of fear. It took months to navigate through their problems, but by asking questions and then listening to her heart, together they built the trust needed to repair their communication conflicts.

Asking questions does not always provide a miraculous resolution to the many troubles that afflict relationships, but the better we understand this tool, the more effectual our questions can be.

Direction and structure

As a psychologist, my focus is communication. More specifically, I encourage others to talk and to open up. For me, questions bring structure and direction to those conversations. Regardless of your employment, questions can greatly assist in bringing coherence, understanding, crystal-clear direction and structure to your work.

Most conversations will take a somewhat random direction unless we follow an established agenda. Even so, conversations often ebb and flow through a number of topics and concepts. With questions, anyone can direct where a conversation is heading. Although not as formal as a meeting agenda, the following simple questions can add structure to the content and direction of a discussion as well as keep us on track and prevent us from pursuing rabbit trails:

- "What are we talking about today?"
- "How much of our time do we want to focus on this one issue?"

Other questions can expand our conversation to head exactly where we want it to go, within agreed parameters:

- "Is that all we are going to talk about?"
- "What other items are vital to talk about today?"

Questions also can cause people to take stock, to second guess their perspectives, or to doubt what they have believed for years. This is called "reasonable doubt."

Reasonable doubt

One of my undergrad instructors was the late Serge Kujawa, a top-ranking crown attorney from Saskatchewan who became a prominent Canadian politician. He came under the international spotlight when he prosecuted Colin Thatcher, a former Saskatchewan cabinet minister, who received a first-degree murder conviction for the 1983 killing of JoAnn Wilson, his former wife. In one of the classes, a student asked Mr. Kujawa if that case was the toughest he ever prosecuted. Serge had many tough cases, yet he did not consider the Thatcher case the toughest. Rather, he said the toughest part of any case was having to prove "beyond a reasonable doubt." Serge further stated that even when a defense attorney provides no real defense, if he asks the right questions, he causes doubt in the minds of the judge or jurors, because the burden of proof lies with the prosecutor. A question merely creates a "reasonable doubt." That's all. Just one logical, viable doubt.

The 1957 movie classic *Twelve Angry Men* starring Henry Fonda is all about a jury, initially deadlocked 11 to 1 in votes that shift to 3 to 9. At that point, Fonda's character of Juror # 8 says, "It's always difficult to keep personal prejudice out of a thing like this. And wherever you run into it, prejudice obscures the truth. I don't really know what the truth is. I don't suppose anybody will ever really know. Nine of us now seem to feel that the defendant is innocent, but we're just gambling on probabilities. We may be wrong. We may be trying to let a guilty man go free, I don't know. Nobody really can. But we have a reasonable doubt, and that's something that's very valuable in our system. No jury can declare a man guilty unless it's sure."

I found that quote applicable to relationships as well. When someone is trapped in a particular way of thinking, you don't need to convince them to accept what you believe. Instead, you just challenge their perspective enough to create doubt, and then their mind will become more open to thinking differently.

In a judicial context, every accused suspect must be proven guilty "beyond a reasonable doubt." Unfortunately, in relationships, we often judge one another, acting both as judge and jury, basing verdicts on events from decades ago. In counselling, many marriages are rescued when accusations are halted; this is done by creating a reasonable doubt. Breaking the cycle of condemnation thinking stops judgmental thinking.

A simple, one-word question often creates reasonable doubt. The question is, "Really?" This six-letter word causes most people to question themselves. When people insert superlative modifiers like, "always," "never," "every," or "totally," those superlatives must be questioned. Asking "Really?" brings the exaggerated statements back into reality. The word levels the playing field. For example, although it sounds like a cliché, I've often heard a spouse complain that their partner never takes out the trash. I respond, "Really? In 18 years of marriage, they have *never* once taken out the garbage?" What the spouse meant to say is that their partner neglected to remove the refuse three or four times in the last month. Reasonable doubt regarding this issue causes the complainer to stop exaggerating and to communicate more honestly. Now we can focus on the real issue: she feels neglected and alone.

I use the principle of "beyond a reasonable doubt" when working with relationships. When a couple is stuck in a rut, even for decades, asking a single question creates a reasonable doubt, changes thinking, and interrupts otherwise negative thought processes, thereby opening the door to unexpected transformation.

Kelly and Carrie were stuck. Like many married couples I have met, they were having the same argument over and over, or another version of the same argument. Kelly had "ruined things" 20 years ago with a one-time marital indiscretion. He had been vilified as "the home wrecker" who made the colossal and unforgivable mistake of cheating on his wife. Carrie, a victim of abuse from her teen years, had never told Kelly about her history until five years after they had been married. Carrie felt perpetually hurt and wounded. Kelly was angry at how cold and distant his wife had become. Many conversations involved Carrie getting frustrated about Kelly's anger and insecurity, and in return, she would react with coldness and unresponsiveness towards him. It was a downward spiral.

In discussion, Carrie actually used the word "unforgivable." I asked her, "Unforgivable? Have you ever forgiven Kelly for this 20-year-old mistake?" My question stopped Carrie in her tracks. Without hesitation she responded, "No, I haven't forgiven him."

The follow-up question was equally as direct: "So, it's okay to lie about your past and not tell your fiancé you were victimized as a teenager?" Their marriage was built on the foundation of half-truths and cover-ups. She could not forgive him for infidelity, but she had expected him to forgive her for not disclosing the whole truth about her background. She was angry, cold, and withdrawn for their first several years of marriage without ever telling him why. He was the "unforgivable" one in her eyes. Her cover-up was fine, but his indiscretion was not.

Both choices were terribly unfortunate. The issue was not about which offence was worse, but rather, it was about a lack of forgiveness. A question stopped the cycle of one-sided negativity and broke the circle of perpetual unforgiveness. By asking Carrie if she had forgiven her husband, it created a reasonable doubt in her view of victimization – that she was not the only victim.

Questions only need to create a reasonable doubt to open the door to a new way of thinking!

Empowerment

When someone asks a question, there is a non-manipulative form of power, depending on who is asking the questions or the motives of the one initiating the conversation. For a well-intentioned leader in the conversation, questions can give power and a sense of control over the direction of the conversation. One should not misguide or unintentionally meander around impressions or feelings. For example, if you ask, "How did you feel about that?" the focus immediately shifts to the thoughts, feelings, and intent of the one being asked. Thus, direction of the conversation rests in the hands of the one who is asking the questions.

To empower a quieter individual with the chance to be heard, ask questions like "Carolyn, did you have anything to say?" or, "Nate, what were your thoughts about this?"

Influence

Beyond taking charge or directing a conversation, questions can be a more compassionate way to communicating. Statements are facts and can become opinionated, judgmental, and divisive, whereas questions usually are not (we will explore this contrast later). You can engage the other participant with questions such as, "So you agree with that?" Now, it is no longer one-sided. While statements put the power and control in the hands of the one asking questions, an opportunity arises to empower those answering. As we give away the power to direct the conversation, we will win influence in return. Control can be wielded with more compassion.

When someone makes the statement, "I don't think our nation should permit any more refugees," lines are drawn in the sand. However, when a wise moderator asks the question, "How can we be reasonably altruistic towards displaced people while still ensuring the safety of our community?" an influence of balance and kindness enters the discussion.

Invitation

In an undirected dialogue, people often wonder, "When is it my turn to speak?" If uninvited, many individuals would rather passively withdraw than assertively fight for an opportunity to speak.

I remember attending a social gathering a few years ago. There were a number of strong personalities in my circle of conversation. I saw a quiet, polite but somewhat shy lady getting bulldozed out of the dialogue. She had neither the energy nor the confidence to compete with type-A conversationalists. At the first opportunity I asked her, "What do you think about that, Donna?" Instantly, she was invited into the spotlight. She shone with great thoughts. Although noticeably intelligent and fully capable of interacting in the conversation, she had been overlooked. One question opened the door for her to step out. In such cases, a question became a platform to invite quieter ones to take center stage.

In a marital conflict, one partner can sometimes dominate the conversation, possibly because they are more vocal and/or outraged by the problem being addressed. This dominating conversationalist has a lot to say about many things. They have no shortage of words or experiences to express their concerns. If they do not notice that their partner has withdrawn and become discouraged, they will continue talking, falsely believing that once they have stated a perspective, the problem is solved.

What the vocal conversationalist may not understand is that when there is no dialogue, the couple will not find an effective resolution to the issue. If the more vocal person observes the behavior of their partner and attends to them by inviting their opinion, not only will greater problems be averted, but current problems will be mutually resolved. Further, the couple will maintain or even increase their love and respect for one another because they experienced mutual satisfaction through the process of the conversation, and listened to each other, even if the desired outcome is not achieved.

Fulfillment

When you ask questions, you are pursuing what you need. My pastor friend Don likes to conclude many of his sermons with a time of questions and answers. He says, "Unfortunately, when I'm preaching, I might answer questions no one is asking. But when I remain quiet to let people ask questions, we are actually having meaningful church." When people ask questions and seek information that concerns them, your answers will help them understand because you are answering questions that relate to them.

What individuals are concerned about is where their energy and attention is directed. Their minds are searching for understanding and closure to an incomplete thought. When they ask a question and the answer is informative, they will learn, accept, retain, and apply the information. Having questions answered results in a sense of fulfillment.

Affirmation

Questions not only lead us toward understanding, they also significantly affirm people. When asking a question, we ask people to communicate. We invite them into dialogue. If I am not interested in your life, I will not ask about it. If I am interested in your life, I will say, "Tell me about you." It is *huge*. What could be more caring than that? It is truly a keystone of communication.

Many people do not make eye contact. Those who do may give a smile or a nod. However, when they smile and engage us, we will wonder about their motive. When we feel safe, we smile back, which may invite a conversation. When people come to my office, I immediately engage them in conversation. Sometimes I start by asking noninvasive, casual questions. This gives my clients the opportunity to make small talk. Such talk provides a level of comfort and familiarity to any new environment that has the potential to feel intimidating. Then, I cautiously explore their reason for attending a counselling session. People usually want to be drawn into a conversation. From my experience, questions are the best way to lead them there. I want people to feel affirmed of their importance as a result of my simple queries.

Care and compassion

When we ask questions, the inclusive component of the conversation says, "You matter, and your opinion matters as well." This approach expresses compassion and builds a relationship. I think about the contrast between the good cop and the bad cop. Bad cop comes as a bully, spewing threats of, "You better tell me or else!" He demands information. For the bad cop, whether literal or metaphorical, in your circle of friends and colleagues, power and intimidation might work, but only for a limited time with limited results. There is no opportunity for repeat business with the bad cop because there is no relational credibility or dynamic. With the good cop, relationship opens the door for ongoing dialogue. The good cop wants to be your friend. He wants the best for you. The bad cop scares you; the good cop cares for you.

The 1970s TV police show *Columbo* featured an abrasive and opinionated detective. Detective Columbo did not come across as warm or caring. He was a black-and-white, no-nonsense guy. As slow, insensitive, bumbling, and rough around the edges as Columbo appeared, he still caused people to feel comfortable even when he was interrogating them, as if they had helped him. Regardless of the witness, he was always able to facilitate a connection because of his approach. Columbo did not use scare tactics, nor was he flowery, gracious, nice, flattering, or patronizing. Columbo was unassuming and nonchalant. He was likeable and affable in an indescribable way. Without fail, Columbo drew the other characters into conversation with his questions.

When an individual feels safe and secure, the exchange becomes meaningful, deep, and honest. The care and compassion do not have to be demonstrative or over the top, but the expression must be sincere. Questions draw people in. Questions not only affirm people, they show people you care.

Can you remember when you had a conversation with someone whom you had just met for the first time? They may have asked how you were enjoying the evening, and how you knew the host of the party. Perhaps they proceeded to ask you about yourself, your work, home, hobbies, and interests. This approach is an inviting way to communicate. Someone cared enough to ask about you. In those moments, you felt cared for. Non-verbal messages such as a smile or nod with accompanying verbal questions led you to interpret and believe that:

- This person likes people.
- This person cares about people.
- This person prefers meaningful dialogue to shallow small talk.
- This person is secure enough to *not* brag about or flaunt things in their own life.

- This person finds people interesting and finds *me* interesting.
- This person wants to know more about others, specifically about *me*.
- This person likes *me*! Great! Someone appreciates who I am.

Demonstrating care and winning credibility in a relationship at the same time is the goal! When you only focus on yourself, you alienate others. Asking questions has historically been identified as one of the best ways to make friends and build relationships.

Obviously, asking questions has some limitations. Asking too many questions, especially personal or intrusive questions, can be invasive and cause discomfort. General inquiry is fine. Interrogation is not.

Comforting confines

The airport in Atlanta is by far the busiest airport in the United States, with around 100 million passengers annually passing through the airport. Navigating a change of gates in that mammoth facility can be daunting. Seven concourses are lettered A – F and T. Each concourse has about 30 to 40 gates. They connect by a central train system that runs from the middle of each of the seven parallel concourses. However, for those unaware, changing from a B gate to a T gate looks to be a 10-mile, multiple hour commute. My friend Mark was already late for a supposedly quick transfer in Atlanta and was anxious about arriving at the gate only moments before his next scheduled flight. To his chagrin, the scheduled flight to his next destination did not match his boarding pass. Frazzled, he headed to the counter and asked where the flight to Calgary was. The agent explained a gate change was posted on the departures board. He had not checked! "Am I too late?" he asked. She smiled and said boarding would begin in 5 minutes on another concourse. "So, I've missed the flight?" he inquired. The helpful agent said, "No, you should be fine." He thought for sure he had missed it. His heart was pounding. He was stressed thinking he would be late for his important engagement in Western Canada.

It was Mark's first time flying through Atlanta. With a couple questions, he managed to get directions, caught the train to the next terminal, and arrived at the departure gate of his connecting flight with moments to spare. A few brief questions brought understanding to an undefined and unclear context. The gate agent brought comfort and security to Mark's situation. Questions bring care as the inquirer asks questions, but questions also bring confines to our human interactions. Boundaries and direction encourage healthy function, congruency, and compatibility in relationships.

Connection

Questions, by nature, unify. They bring people together. In a conversation riddled with questions, there are invitations to think, process, and respond.

Perhaps you have heard the phrase "ABCs of relationship building," which refers to the terms Ascertain Affinity, Building Bridges, Communication and Conversation. This is used as a business template and sales language for engaging business associates. The system helps businesses move toward a more relational paradigm - less "results driven" or "bottom-line" focused and more "people focused." Ultimately, caring for people around you and in business, leads to a greater sense of wellbeing in the workplace, thereby improving long-term business and profits. However, clients easily discern an overemphasis on profit. Focusing on building relationship shifts from selfishness to authentic interest in people.

Consequently, when people feel valued and cared for and sense that you are not just after their money, they commit to long-term relationship and repeated sales. Conversely, high-pressure sales and sensational advertising may reap short-term benefits, but in the long run, it's a "one and done" method of marketing and it predominates with poor long-term results.

Chapter 4

Questions teach

"No one can teach, if by teaching we mean the transmission of knowledge, in any mechanical fashion, from one person to another. The most that can be done is that one person who is more knowledgeable than another can, by asking a series of questions, stimulate the other to think, and so cause him to learn for himself."

– Socrates, 5th century BC

Questions, obviously, serve to illicit information. Well-asked questions stretch the mind and make us think rather than just memorize information. They function in the role of a thought-provoking teacher.

Questions and circumstances

Extremes often point out principles not otherwise visible to the naked eye. To better understand what questions accomplish, let's look at one of the more extreme examples from my line of work. I have done a significant amount of work with post-traumatic stress disorder (PTSD) and stress debriefing. One of the trainings I received was called critical incidents stress debriefing. In this course, I was taught that there are basically three simple questions to ask victims of trauma in a debriefing session. The research, we were told, indicated that the sooner a traumatized individual processed their experience (i.e., debriefed), the less likely they were to experience significant long-term effects of PTSD. Sometimes these questions are asked to soldiers after experiencing a combat situation, a victim of a crime, or a witness of a tragic event.

The three questions are:

1. "What did you see or what happened?" This question deals with the **facts**.
2. "What did you feel about it?" This question deals with the **feelings**.
3. "How has this event impacted you?" This question deals with the **future**.

Without these questions, facts and feelings become suppressed, unprocessed, and unresolved. Questions unlock the door to begin the healing journey.

I know a fighter pilot who flew many missions during the Vietnam War. He had never told his story about the war – such as getting shot down or other experiences – until recently. On every flight, there was a co-pilot. The planes flew in pairs, two planes going out on every mission with the same pilots and co-pilots. On what was to be his last sortie, he was hit fairly significantly, barely making it home alive. The other pilots made it home as well, all physically unharmed. However, all of them were emotionally harmed. After four decades, three simple questions led to profound healing for this gentleman who had locked away volumes of his life's story.

Whether the trauma was decades or days ago, the issues need be processed to prevent pain, loss, grief, and unresolved emotion from settling in. Discussing his previously unspoken events brought this pilot significant closure. Emotions and memories do *not* just magically disappear because the event is over and he is now home. Unwittingly, our society emotionally assaults victims of trauma with the message, "Just get over it!" Questions give these traumatized individuals permission to process their life-altering events.

The same rules apply within a marriage. Together, couples face numerous events and issues. Some issues can be emotionally heightened while some are traumatic. The three questions cited above bring healing and improve marriages, not only for those who have experienced severe trauma. Questions help us process life events rather than falsely thinking we'll "just get over it" and our marriages will miraculously improve. We must allow questions to teach important life lessons as we attend to our issues.

For example, the effects of stress caused by unresolved emotional issues, trauma, or other problems can build up in the body, producing symptoms of muscle tension or pain, elevated blood pressure, gain or loss of weight, or sleep disturbances. There are other possible effects and expressions that can indicate an increase of stress. Eventually, it takes a physical toll on the body. During these periods of stress, the body needs to be attended to. If we are not asking why the body is feeling what it is, things can get worse. The same can be said of a relationship under stress or in crises. There are indicators and they require attention.

How statements affect communication

Most dictionaries define "statement" as "an expression or an account of facts or events." Although a succinct and expeditious means of conveyance, such factual expressions can accompany a vast array of emotion, judgment, assumption, ridicule, and condescension.

What exactly do statements accomplish? Statements present facts and expose a person's point of view. They tend to be one-sided and often do not invite others into the conversation. Heavily opinionated statements can easily alienate others or evoke negative emotions, especially in emotionally charged situations. In the context of relationship, especially during conflict, statements can perpetrate swift and deep damage.

Trevor, a rather outspoken man, had little tact or sensitivity. Michelle, his wife, was the daughter of a drug-abusing father who verbally bullied her for as long as she could remember. Their marriage and her confidence level were perpetually eroding under Trevor's destructive statements, such as "Well, that's stupid" or "That's no good!" I witnessed this narrative for the first 15 minutes of our initial appointment. Most guys are on their "best behavior" while sitting in the marriage counsellor's office. Not Trevor. By the midway point of our session, after he had expressed many judgments, we agreed on ground rules that labeled such negativity as "out of bounds," both at counselling appointments and as a life rule. His repeated negative statements were ruining both their marriage and Michelle's wellbeing. Each statement was like a hand grenade blowing up their marital happiness and serenity.

Think of a disagreement you had with your spouse, a co-worker, or a close friend. Can you remember things getting heated, the adrenaline starting to flow, emotions beginning to rise as conflict emerged? Managing conflict or differing opinions is a vital component to any healthy relationship. It is not appropriate to disregard or write people off any time they have thoughts different from ours. We cannot live our lives cloistered away from everyone else. Instead, we should be open to the unique opinions of others without ending the relationship over a dissimilar position, even when it stirs up tension, discomfort, or uneasiness. In those moments, questions can build a bridge to a healthier relationship, or we can drop a bomb in the form of a negative statement. As the conflict escalates and feelings make their way into conversation, "bombs" get dropped bringing hurt into the dialogue. For example:

- "That's dumb!"
- "You're an idiot!"
- "You *always* do that."
- "I used to think that, back when I was immature."
- "You've messed things up again, like the time when…"
- "This is *all* your fault!"
- "*You've* got a problem."
- "I don't know if I can stay in a relationship with someone who thinks like this!"
- "I hate you."
- "You're lying."
- "That's not true!"

These statements intensify a disagreement and cause individuals to build divisive walls that ultimately destroy the relationship's vitality. Although questions can easily be inappropriate and hurtful (such as "What is your problem?"), a well-timed question can quickly build bridges to move us towards resolution, instead of destruction.

The content of a statement is subjective and often personal to the one who shares. Most statements we make are based on experiences, learning, and personal reflections. It is likely the easiest and most natural way of communicating, where we just tell it like it is. Who among us does not like to share their own thoughts or theories? However, as we mingle in our feelings, opinions, and emotionally charged concerns, statements instantly move beyond a neutral presentation of fact to what the old TV westerns used to call "fightin' words." Those fightin' words never start out as fightin' words, but when we live with people in close proximity (work, home, or marriage), feelings can escalate quickly. As couples share their lives together, the issue is not *if* conflict will arise, but *when* and how frequently conflict will happen.

Successful marriages are comprised of two individuals who have learned to handle conflict graciously and will lovingly strive to communicate well. Success does not happen magically, quickly, or easily. Good communication skills are developed through painstaking process, often through trial and error and with a willingness to compromise in light of enduring commitment.

Questions can interrupt our current way of thinking

Have you ever been hit hard by some difficult news? We try to function normally after we hear a medical diagnosis of a family member, the loss of a job, or the death of a loved one. We try to carry on with our day-to-day routines to get through those times of crisis.

Do you remember a time you were burdened by such bad news that you just switched to autopilot, didn't engage with others, couldn't cope, and detached for the most part? Can you recall the subsequent two or three days after hearing the bad news when a friend asked a caring question? Perhaps they asked, "Hey, you don't seem yourself. How are you, really?" rather than the, "Hey, how are you?" question typically heard in casual conversation.

Earlier this year, a friend received a sobering medical diagnosis that caused initial alarm. Although not an immediate crisis, the possible long-term outcomes included potential fatality. He stayed busy through the next week or so, talking a bit about it, but not fully processing the emotional weight of it. The following week, a close friend who was aware of the situation connected with him. The friend looked him in the eye, paused, then asked two quick, direct questions: "Hey, have you had any more reports from the doctor? How are you doing with all this?" The change of pace in the dialogue, the gentle tone of voice, and the questions themselves showed my friend that someone cared about him. In response, my friend teared up as he conveyed the most recent update. Two questions had conveyed care and empathy simply because they were asked with sincere compassion.

Questions can create cooperation

We ask questions to offer an expression of mutual engagement. The one who asks a question creates an environment for a voluntary encounter; it is about building a culture of cooperation. Without questions, conversations can easily be dominated by "conversation bullies." Have you ever been in a group dominated by a strong voice and wondered, "When will it be my turn to share?" Have you felt minimized because the incessant talking bully has indirectly inferred, "I will talk and you will listen"?

When I ask you a question, I am saying that your opinion matters. I'm cooperating with you. I want *you* to engage with *me* in dialogue. Even when the answer is different than what I was expecting, a meaningful dialogue occurs because there is an exchange of questions and answers. Your answers to my questions help me to understand you and your perspective. Even if you do not get to answer in a group context, the answer you formulate in your mind engages my question; therefore we have engaged each other even if words are not spoken. That is the spirit of cooperation.

"Why" questions

"Why" can be an ugly question. When "why" is used to answer another question originally asked or when "why" is asked following a statement, it can be misinterpreted. Misunderstanding especially arises from emails or texts as there is no tone or facial expression to help interpret.

For example, asking "why" questions can:

- be interpreted as a challenge;
- be misconstrued as a judgment;
- be an expression of doubt;
- seem threatening;
- imply that your statement or response was insufficient;
- be misinterpreted by implying that someone is inferior, childlike, or that you need to explain your actions or thoughts;
- imply that your thinking is flawed, or even *you* perhaps are flawed;
- imply that you are being unreasonable; or
- imply that you don't deserve such a positive outcome.

Asking "why" can be offensive when the individual being asked does not know or understand the motivation behind the question. "Why" questions can quickly be associated with a negative reason for asking. They can be intimidating, uninviting, or feel judgmental. They sometimes make people feel threatened. Repeatedly asking "why?" suggests the answers heard are not good enough. In these circumstances, "why?" does not encourage or feel compassionate.

Consider these examples:

Scenario #1

Wife: "I was in bed early last night. What time did you get in?"
Husband: "11:30 p.m."
Wife: "Why?"

The wife may genuinely be concerned for her husband. She might think, "Was everything alright? Did he get a flat tire? Was there a problem somewhere?" But if there is any history of suspicion or mistrust, the defensive husband could escalate the discussion by retorting, "You don't trust me! I wasn't with anyone! What is wrong with you?" Although she only asked a one-word question, it can be readily and frequently misunderstood.

Scenario #2

Husband (text message to wife): "Did you remember to buy a gift for Anna's birthday?"
Wife (text response to husband): "I most certainly did! I picked up a coffee gift card while I was at the drug store so she can buy five of her favorite lattés."

Husband (text response): "Why?"

The wife then sends her husband an angry emoticon and puts her phone on airplane mode.

Without realizing, the wife assumed her husband's "why?" meant there was something wrong with her gift selection. By questioning the gift, he unknowingly implied that it was not good enough, lacking in some way, or perhaps too generous.

The back story is they had discussed it in passing two days before. The idea to email a gift card had come up since Anna's birthday was in two days but they would not see her for two weeks. The husband had a spare minute and was wondering if he should order it online or if his wife had already done that. He was just asking why his wife had purchased a physical gift card instead of emailing one Anna would get on time for her birthday. He was not angry. However, it seemed that way to his wife.

That's a great question

A statement from the 18th century philosopher Voltaire suggests we should judge a man by his questions instead of his answers. Contemporary versions of this old truth suggest that we judge a man's intelligence by his questions more than his answers. There may be some truth to this thought.

Have you known someone who is successful because of an ability to ask great questions? They seem to ask the right questions at the right time to bring clarity. They appear to embrace learning. They seem teachable. As their understanding grows with each question, so does the understanding and clarity of those around them. They often hear the comment, "That's a great question!" As a result, they are invited into numerous conversations. Their inquisitive, teachable nature makes them a welcome addition to any dialogue. For some, asking great questions is a natural talent. Others work hard to learn this skill. Both can become successful through these means.

Questions can create neutrality

Questions level the playing field. In a relationship, we are easily held hostage by the one expressing anger. The tension created by the angry or anxious person dominates the conversation. They appear to be in control while everyone else walks on eggshells. The dynamic in the relationship fundamentally exposes underlying issues.

What is the reason for the statement that was just made? A few clarifying questions create a context of neutrality and a leveling out of tensions. Questions have the uncanny ability to bring issues to the surface, thereby exposing and neutralizing motivations.

In the biblical story of Creation, God has an encounter with Adam shortly after humankind is created. Although God is described as omniscient or all-knowing, His first recorded conversation with man finds God asking a question! It may seem odd that an all-knowing God would ask a question. Why would He seek an answer that He already knows?

This is the genius of questions. Questions bring truth and understanding to the conversation, even when the answer is already known. Pretty clever!

As Adam and Eve are wallowing in their shame of disobedience, God asks, "Where are you?" (Genesis 3:9). The next three sentences that God uses to engage the dialogue are all inquiries.

Similarly, in another biblical story, God is found conversing with Adam's son Cain. God exposed Cain's hidden issues before and after the first murder in history – the killing of his brother, Abel. Eternally seeking to restore relationship between Himself and humankind as well as between humans, God perpetually asks questions, as noted in the books of the Prophets. Although God knows the answer to the questions He asks, He does this to reveal truth, expose hidden motivations, and get to the bottom of issues. This is called accountability. In a relational context, the more noble, higher goal is to improve communication and thereby bring truth, love, and justice to the forefront – all of which can be accomplished through questions.

A couple had not been in my office more than five minutes when the raging husband stormed out, leaving his wife in tears. She was conflicted because she desperately wanted to go after him, to chase him down. In reality, he did not want to be there. Not at all. Although she had managed to get him to the counselling session, he would not stay. He was not interested in deepening his relationship with his wife. For this gentleman, with just a couple questions, the truth came out. He finally said, "This is the kind of relationship I want. I'm not interested in going any deeper."

Ultimately, this wife had to decide, "How do I stay faithful in this marriage when I feel so disconnected? Can I choose to be satisfied with this level of relationship? Can I make deeper connections with friends to compensate?" Her expectations were significantly modified. She realized that the emotional connection she needed had to be satisfied through her kids and her friends. She could have remained in denial with her husband and pretended that everything was satisfactory, but it wasn't. She was courageous enough to find that level of understanding by asking, "What do we have in this relationship?" She could have spent the rest of her life second-guessing herself, reacting all the time, but that would be a miserable existence for her. She decided to stay after coming to the realization that she had good, intimate friendships that would fill the void. We can pretend, or we can accept the reality and adjust to it.

To be at peace, we must settle the unresolved issues in our minds. The uncertainty can be frustrating. Questions may not bring immediate solutions, but they do bring a measure of clarity and, consequently, neutrality. The confusion of not understanding or not knowing can lead to health issues and emotional instability as we continually ask ourselves, "What is this really about? Can I achieve peace?" It is hard to guess what each day will look like or what the future will hold when you are trying to figure out what is going on. The reality is that we may never fully understand or be able to "fix" the situation. Instead, can we adjust or be okay with lowering our expectations?

Questions can change the course of control

When I observe a conversation between two people, it sometimes reminds me of a tennis match: back and forth, back and forth. When more people are involved in the communication, everybody has a comment, a thought, an idea, or an opinion to contribute. When conversations escalate into arguments, such outbursts can expose true perspectives and feelings, or create more confusion with no clarity in sight. That is the journey of communication between people; we do not know how it will go or where it will end up.

It would be wonderful if we had an agenda or script to follow every time we had a conversation so that every participant got an equal share of floor time. Even more helpful would be a moderator to govern each step of the dialogue and ensure that fair play rules the day and feelings are respectfully expressed. But that is not always possible.

Questions, however, provide us with infinite possibilities for direction for fair and healthy guidelines and, as a result, a measure of order and control. Even in emotionally volatile situations, questions like the following can be very productive:

- "What ground rules do we need for this discussion?"
- "If we don't accept what the other person is saying, can we commit to thinking the best about each other?"
- "As we chat about this emotionally charged issue, can we keep the focus on the topic instead of the person?"
- "Can we agree that whatever we discuss will be held in confidence?"
- "Can we commit to follow through with whatever we agree on?"
- "Is there anything else we need to agree on first?"

After a season of instability, a business began asking these exact questions to establish a code of conduct. It intentionally created a new corporate culture. Imagine how much better a discussion, even a heated discussion, might ensue when you ask questions beforehand to establish boundaries. Questions are a game changer as well as a culture changer.

Well-placed, well-timed, well-thought-out questions bring more control to conversations. Those caught in the back-and-forth tennis match of comments do not need to become victims of random statements. Such random thoughts, opinions, and concepts can unpredictably appear at inopportune times. The inquirer, especially a caring and strategically intentional inquirer, can bring a significant level of direction, focus, flow, and resolution into any discussion. A strong facilitator in a meeting does not need to make a single statement to redirect a troubled agenda into smoother sailing. In a group setting where conversation is normally dominated by the strongest voice, even the quietest voice can be heard when called upon by the one who wisely directs questions. The out-of-control meeting can quickly get back *in* control.

Rick, who chairs a local not-for-profit organization, is a bull-in-a-china-shop kind of leader. Kevin, who was just elected to the board, is much more of a collegial team player. As a result, Kevin grits his teeth every time Rick powers through another item on the agenda without consulting others on the board. Rick is quick to share his own opinions, often with a heaping dose of belligerence and passion, thereby wasting considerable time in the process. Kevin, a savvy leader, knows he does not need the chairmanship to influence a meeting. With an articulate, confident voice, Kevin speaks to an agenda item succinctly, then immediately brings others into the conversation: "But what do you think, Cheryl? Do you agree or disagree with my thoughts on that, Greg?" By asking questions, Kevin wins the favor of his peers. They already have agreed among themselves that when the current chairman's term ends, they will ask Kevin to lead the board. People admire leaders who ask questions because these leaders value the input of others.

When questions are not asked

Conversations without questions, especially emotionally charged ones, become a free-for-all with no boundaries or parameters. Opinions and statements fly around the room unchecked, leading to a chaotic release of opinions and feelings. Discussions quickly escalate into a mean-spirited fight. There are strong opinions about *everything*, even about the person and who they are, not just what they have done. It is no longer about the issue; it is personal. Emotions like hurt, anger, and frustration become the focus of attack. Character assassination becomes the order of the day. Someone will inevitably be offended. It is no longer about the facts but about "how I feel and I am going to make sure you know it." Other than burning bridges, is anything accomplished?

Craig Hill, author of *Ancient Paths*, writes about levels of conversation present in our homes that you cannot see, like a wi-fi signal. He calls the first level of conversation the "topical" level. The second, just beneath but more important, is the "relational" level. Your wife might say, "It's not what you said, but the way you said it" (relational level). The husband responds, "You always take what I say the wrong way and then you criticize me" (topical level). The topic is discussed, but the relationship, the deeper issues of the heart, might be ignored.

Allow me to stereotype: women tend to be more focused on the relationship, thoughts, and feelings, so they function at the relational level; men are generally task-oriented, so they hear the topic and function at a topical level. Since men often talk about a topic, they seldom consider deeper relational concerns. When the conversation becomes emotionally heightened, they often fail to approach the topic. Instead, they talk about insignificant issues that overlook the real issue – the enduring relational concerns.

Perhaps you remember seeing a comedic dialogue that appeared during the early days of the Internet, depicting thoughts and conversation between a couple. Let me try to recount it here:

In a living room, a married couple is sitting on a sofa. She thinks, *"He hasn't said anything for five minutes. His brow is furrowed. He seems deep in thought. I wonder if he's bothered about what I said last week about needing to take our relationship to a deeper level?"*

She finally says, "Honey, what are you thinking?"

He thinks, *"I wonder if there is a ball game on this afternoon?"*

With his brow furrowed, he finally says, "Nothing."

She thinks to herself, *"He is upset. I knew it. I feel tension in the room. He never talks about his feelings. I need to draw him out. I need to get him to open up."* She reaches out to him, caresses his arm, then rests her hand on his shoulder. She smiles and looks fondly into his eyes as her hand warmly strokes the back of his neck.

She asks, "What are you thinking about?" Then, with a hint of concern, "Honey?"

"Yeah," he says. "I was just thinking about the credit card statement coming in soon. We have a lot of bills piling up and I need to stay on top of things."

She thinks, *"He's guarded. I can feel it. He's hiding something."* She asks, "Are you bothered by anything that we have talked about?"

He thinks, *"Oh no! I have no idea what to say!"* He freezes, then there is a long, awkward pause.

She thinks, *"He can't open up. Does he care about me at all?"*

He thinks, *"Yeah. When is that credit card statement coming in? What's going to be on that statement this month? What nice thing could I say?"*

He then says, "Honey, I've been thinking. We should start taking walks together." He gives her a loving hug and they smile at each other.

She thinks, *"It's not over. He loves me. He cares about me. He hears me. He has been listening all along."*

Truly, the gender disparity easily explains why people joke that men and women are from different planets! She thinks and communicates on a relational level; he thinks and communicates on a topical level. In the previous story, even though she is asking questions, she is moving in a relational plane of thought, while the husband is stuck on a topic. Her questions assume he is on the same page of relational thought. How does this difference in thinking affect our relationships? She asks general questions like, "What are you thinking?" presuming he is thinking about their relationship, yet, in reality, he is only thinking about the credit card statement and non-relational points.

In this dialogue, many thoughts and ideas are assumed. Many couples sit in my office flinging accusations about one another that are based on false assumptions. For example, "He never listens to me, never hears me." Frequently, the response from a spouse is defensive, emotional, and accusatory. "Really?! That's because you never hear me!" Each wants to know how their partner feels, and the negative emotions need to be processed. It is important to give enough weight to the issue rather than blame the other for their feelings. Unfortunately, I have seen hundreds of conversations deteriorate because the emotion becomes the center of the conversation while the actual issue is ignored.

A healthier dialogue

Thankfully, there is a healthier way to dialogue. There is a better way to bring thoughts to the surface. One could help their partner by asking questions like, "What can I do to facilitate improved communication?" or, "Would you give me feedback about what I am concerned about?" In a healthy conversation, we own what we think and feel, not what others assume we think and feel. Conversation based on presumption is dangerous. The more emotionally charged the conversation, the greater the increase of misunderstanding and pain.

Helping, or fixing?

When couples have a heated conversation, some communicate by using "I" statements, such as, "I feel frustrated" or "I feel angry" or "I feel that's not fair." These statements of personal feelings reinforce the reason why they are addressing an issue. In sharing emotions, they no longer feel powerless in the situation. However, they can easily fall into the trap of taking the blame when their partner starts to share how they feel. They can share their feelings, but then feel blamed when their partner shares their feelings in return. Each one must consciously and intentionally make an effort to avoid getting defensive, withdrawing, or feeling guilty. It is not up to the communicator to change the partner's feelings or to fix them. Instead, there is a responsibility to listen, respect, and understand. Such revelation helps each to not get caught up in the feelings, but to focus on resolving the issue. It comes down to making the relationship better. Do not discount the feelings of your partner, but set boundaries. We are not each other's emotional managers. We just want to understand the feelings. The best way to understand each other is to ask questions. At the end of the day, we are each responsible for our own feelings. We are not responsible to fix the other person's feelings.

I will never fully understand my wife. I will never fully understand anyone for that matter. And no one will ever fully understand me. That's okay! No one really fully understands all of the feelings communicated – even when others are doing an exceptional job of sharing their emotions. That is not the point. Complete understanding is not the goal. The point is to help the relationship. In any discussion, you cannot make the other person feel what you have felt. You cannot make them pay for what you have felt. I can genuinely appreciate how you feel as you describe your story to me to the best of your ability. Once I hear and acknowledge those feelings, the most important response is, "How can we help the relationship to be better equipped moving forward?" We might not be able to eliminate the pain, but we can improve the relationship dynamics.

Chapter 5

Better understanding

"When people talk, listen completely.
Most people never listen."
– Ernest Hemingway

The understanding of Solomon and *Tool Time*

King Solomon, the Hebrew King who ruled 3000 years ago, is regarded as the wisest man who ever lived. He believed that life's goal, whatever the cost, was to get understanding.

King Solomon did not think of understanding as an isolated concept, but rather a triumvirate of knowledge, understanding, and wisdom – all three together. When he spoke of knowledge, he was often referring to the accumulation of facts. However, it was not just about facts or knowledge, nor was it merely about knowing what to do with that knowledge. It was about coming to a place of understanding that went *beyond* knowledge.

For Solomon, understanding meant having insight about how to unite hearts and minds. When he spoke of wisdom, he was speaking of knowing what to do with the accumulated knowledge and understanding as well as when to use that knowledge and understanding. Knowing when to engage a conversation or how to say what you want to say is very important. Wisdom is more important than just spewing out what you know, understand, believe, or feel. If your information or perspective is shared when another individual is not ready to listen, or if expressed in an uncaring or nonemphatic manner, the relationship could sustain significant damage. King Solomon saw a level of moral responsibility and good living that came with such wisdom. Consequently, Solomon encouraged people to pursue that kind of knowledge, that plane of wisdom, and the place of understanding – no matter what the cost!

In perusing various dictionaries to define understanding, there is a recurring theme. The first definition of understanding usually includes synonyms like comprehension, a mental grasp, or other words that imply "getting it" intellectually. Beyond those basic definitions of understanding, many dictionaries include a second or third definition with a relational component, such as:

- Accepting people's behavior and forgiving them
- Being sympathetic towards other people's feelings
- Being forgiving and tolerant
- Having compassion or sympathy

Understanding, then, not only embodies intellectual assent as being "in the know," but also incorporates a broad spectrum of responses, including a measure of kindness and grace to be expressed in the context of feeling and emotion.

Unfortunately, much of our lives are filled with misunderstanding. Comedian Tim Allen, who played the character Tim Taylor in the 1990s sitcom *Home Improvement*, was very familiar with misunderstanding. The painfully recurring theme of misunderstanding was highlighted in every episode. Tim loved his wife Jill without doubt, but he often said and did the wrong things, which always came back to bite him before the end of the show.

The show followed a kind of formula. Tim is an accident-prone guy, stereotypical of everything wrong with sports and tool-loving men, and he is also a bit unmindful and oblivious to the needs of his wife. Jill, the long-suffering patient wife, is always forgiving. Although a devout husband and father, Tim inevitably repeats big mistakes and is misunderstood by his wife and kids. He perpetually confides in Wilson, his sagely neighbor, for advice and then proceeds to butcher the prescribed relationship wisdom. He routinely apologizes to his wife and ultimately makes amends.

When feeling uncomfortable, Tim consistently misinterprets or misstates commonly understood beliefs, phrases, colloquialisms, myths, or even book titles in an effort to sound intelligent or to be funny. In one episode, Tim and Jill attend a marriage therapy workshop, although with great reluctance from Tim. Tim feels anxious and tries to make light of the frequent difficult emotional moments by injecting what he thinks are funny comments.

At the time when this episode was recorded, a popular book titled *Men are from Mars, Women are from Venus* *was* in circulation. Tim's character on *Home Improvement* was host of the fictional show *Tool Time* where he demonstrated how to use various tools. As Tim related everything in life to tools, he made a snarky comment comparing marriage maintenance to tool maintenance: "You must have heard that hammers are from Venus and pliers are from Mars." This comment caused Jill to become embarrassed and unhappy.

While ranked as an above-average American sitcom, the life of Tim Taylor becomes unfortunate and painful for real life, as misunderstanding brings much pain to real relationships. Good understanding, communication, and conversation contribute to a healthy relationship and a more satisfying life.

Find a way to relate

The ABCs of business relationships propagated years ago were simple:

- Ascertain affinity: Ask questions to find common ground with the client
- Build bridges: Transition from common ground to where you want to go
- Communication and conversation: Talk about the client and the product

Conversationally share from your own experiences how this product has made your life better and will ultimately make their lives better - especially since you, the sales person, and them, the client, have things in common.

Marketers, advertisers, sales people, and companies were forced to embrace these simple truths that not only reflected the relational paradigm but also the long-term value in customer relationships because brand loyalty had diminished. Without a personal connection, people would no longer purchase appliances from their favorite department store just because their parents and grandparents did.

Years ago, a home furnishing store started a trend by advertising that you could purchase a "house full of furniture for just $2,000" and you wouldn't pay for a year. The sales strategy was not based on high pressure or the wonderful warranty and service provided. The appeal was in deferred payment, a great low price, and reliable product quality. The sales people did not pressure customers in the store. They asked about sports, weather, and where customers travelled on vacation; they wanted some point of connection to establish relationship. As they built a bridge of connection, they built trust. The really good sales people asked the right questions, found what they had in common with the client, and chatted it up. After a few minutes of conversation, each gained a sense of connection. Perhaps you both visited the same vacation spot, and the salesman stayed at a hotel just down the road from where you stayed. In less than three minutes of inquiry, you had practically become neighbors. How could any customer not trust a guy like that?

The take-away from the salesperson's questions was the value placed on relationships and the power of asking questions to build the relationships. To be sure, the depth of relationship in this instance was superficial, but the importance of relationship was demonstrated through the connection created by the inquiry of the salesperson. A skilled professional and genuinely caring salesperson could show enough interest in a client to establish an environment of perceived community, a sense of connectedness. Some salespersons could have faked these traits and established a false environment simply to facilitate a sale, but the truly authentic and compassionate salesperson raised the bar on how to *relate* and *sell* at the same time. Thus, the perspective that produced repeat customers boiled down to this: "When we care about people, the bottom line will take care of itself."

These sales principles have taught us to prioritize meaningful and caring relationships. For those who highly value relationships, asking questions is a natural expression of two-sided conversations because it establishes care, kindness, sincerity, and authenticity. I am certain the idea of "caring enough to ask" can be applied to everyday conversations. We must move beyond merely knowing surface information about people to an in-depth connection.

Chapter 6

A little help from science

"It is not that I'm so smart. But I stay
with the questions much longer."
– Albert Einstein

For me, it's such a privilege to journey through the counselling process with dozens of clients every week.`Where personal and relational roadblocks once seemed hopeless, it's fulfilling and rewarding to watch gradual improvements result from a proper line of questioning that brings change. I have seen firsthand how questions can turn relationships around. I have anecdotal support of hundreds of times where the right question allowed me to challenge thinking, stimulate further conversation, and see individuals come to a point of understanding, acceptance, and change.

It is encouraging to see people transformed through the power of questions. This transformation holds even more significance when you understand what happens neurologically and biologically as questions are asked.

Science helps us understand just how vital questions are. The complementary concepts of mindfulness and metacognition move us toward a greater understanding of how the mind grows and develops.

Mindfulness

Mindfulness as a psychological term means exactly what you would expect. It means being present in the moment, being alert, aware, and conscious of the internal and external stimuli.

When we are aware of what we and those around us are thinking and feeling, we are better prepared to engage in more meaningful discussions and ask questions that are deeper and more intelligent than, "What did you do today?" If we are proceeding in mindfulness, the skill level of our questions incorporates the feelings of the moment as well as historical and future considerations as they all pertain to those in our immediate sphere of conversation. We engage in the lives of others by understanding their contexts. We move beyond small talk into mindful, meaningful dialogue.

Metacognition

Beyond mindfulness lies the similar but even deeper concept known as metacognition. Simply put, cognition means "thinking." The Greek word "meta" is occasionally used as an English prefix. In the ancient Greek "meta" means any of the following: after, behind, changed, beyond, or higher. In the context of metacognition, "meta" refers to thinking higher, or thinking beyond. The term "metacognition" simply means "thinking about thinking" or "thinking about thoughts."

For example, I could be thinking about the errands I have to do on the way home from work; I need to get to the bank because I need to pay a bill immediately; I should stop at the dry cleaners and then go to the grocery store for a few items. However, thinking deeper, I reason that I should go to the grocery store first, then the dry cleaners, and finally the bank because that is the most direct route with no backtracking. To think even deeper would be to ponder, "Why was I thinking about the bank first? I must be a bit stressed or obsessed with that bill payment. I should relax. I've had the bill for a week, but it isn't due for another week." This thinking at a deeper level includes self-awareness and perhaps even self-monitoring that allows us to grow and develop in our thought processes.

When we ask questions, we create an opportunity to move our conversations from basic reacting thoughts and opinions to a deeper metacognitive level. There are many questions we could ask that would cause us to think about our thoughts. When overwhelmed by a negative emotion, we should ask ourselves, "Why am I feeling this way? What thoughts am I thinking that could cause me to feel this way?" Likewise, we could ask others questions such as, "Can you please help me understand your thoughts about that?" to hopefully avoid an emotionally charged exchange. Or, a question like, "I want to hear you better. Can you unpack that for me?" can quickly adjust the emotional thermostat in the room. By doing this, we are not only mindful that there is conflict in the conversation, but we are even willing to dig deeper into, "How is my current way of thinking hurting our conversation? And how can I change my thoughts, feelings, and actions right now?"

When we move into that depth of conversation, we not only react with emotion but also respond with our minds as well. We are not obliged to respond on an instinctive, defensive level. Instantaneously, when we move into metacognition, our emotions subside. Theoretically, when we become more aware of our thoughts and emotions, we gain control and management of our emotions and behaviors.

Martin and Tracy were in my office working on marriage issues when Tracy stated, "Martin never listens to me." I could see Martin become agitated. I have heard dozens of responses to statements just like that; suffice to say, few of them are positive. Things usually escalate quickly and deteriorate even quicker and I find myself refereeing a yelling match. So, I stepped in.

"Hold on a second, Tracy," I interjected. "Do you mean to tell me that Martin *never* listens to you?" Martin started to nod in a kind of yeah-take-that sort of way. He seemed pleased that I took his side for once.

"No, I can't think of a single time I've opened my mouth that he listened to me!" she retorted.

"So," I continued, "Have you asked him to clean up the dishes any time this last month, or drive you or the kids somewhere, or cut the grass, or pick up a few things at the grocery store, run other errands...any of those kind of things?"

"Well, okay, yeah, he's done some of that stuff, but that's not what I mean," she said backing off a bit. I could see Martin was simmering and smoldering significantly less.

I pushed for clarity, "So he *has* listened to you about some things, Tracy? What kind of things has he *not* been listening to you about? To you, it feels like he's heard nothing, but he's heard some things very well. What things is he *not* hearing?" Tracy thought about her words for a moment. She started thinking about her thoughts and feelings. She had been gently challenged. She realized she needed to change it up and communicate differently. She had been harsh and abrupt and confrontational because she was hurt.

"You know, personal things," she offered, a little less guarded, somewhat vulnerable.

"No, I don't know," I responded. I had an idea, but did not want to assume for Martin's sake. "What kind of things is Martin not hearing? He's hearing something."

"I'm sorry," she said softly. "Martin, you've actually done really well lately, getting stuff done around the house, helping clean up, helping with the kids more, I'm very grateful…" Martin had completely softened at this point. His body language changed, he actually leaned toward his wife, and his arms unfolded and rested by his side. His defenses came down as she said, "…but it's my feelings you're not acknowledging."

"What?" said an unbelieving Martin. "I hear you. I hear your frustration about work, about your boss, about your mom, about the problem with the driveway being repaired poorly. I hear all that. I know you're frustrated." Tracy teared up. Martin looked at me and shrugged, not really sure what to do. Tracy continued, "Yeah, yeah, that's some of the stuff, but do you hear what I feel? What I think?" Martin was wide-eyed and terrified as she went on. However, his defenses were down so that he could hear his wife say, "I'm lonely. I'm all alone. I try to talk to you, but you don't hear me. You're distant. You're here but you're not here. You're tuned out." Martin looked somewhere on the spectrum between clueless and horrified.

I asked Martin what he just heard Tracy say. "Uh. I need to be home more?"

"No, Martin. What did your wife just say? What emotions did she just convey?" Martin was not equipped to handle his wife's emotions. He mostly froze up any time she shared her feelings. "She's lonely?" he asked, hoping it was the right answer. Martin was truly in unchartered territory. He had the information but he had no idea what to do with it. He wanted to help. He didn't know how!

I know this seems incredibly obvious, but I asked Martin, "How does that make you feel?"

"Sad," Martin said.

"Anything else?" I asked.

"No, just sad," he said again, hoping to have another feeling, but that's all he could come up with.

"Is there something you want to say to Tracy?" I prompted.

"Tracy I'm very sorry that you're feeling lonely.... um, I'm here. I want to be here for you. I came to counselling, right?" Martin blundered along still somewhat defensive. And then he stumbled onto something, probably quite by accident, when he stated, "And I want to be your best friend, and I want to help you and hear you." He took her hand and looked her in the eye and said, "I'm committed to you. I love you." He was sincere. He was actually engaged in the moment. Things did not escalate. They were not yelling. They both thought about how they thought and communicated on a metacognitive level, or at least were being mindful of each other. A few simple clarifying questions led them to think about the usual thought processes of accusation, defensiveness, and yelling. As they finally thought about each other in the moment, the normal adversarial emotions dissipated.

Neurological response

In that heated moment between Martin and Tracy, their minds and bodies and emotions started to react as they had dozens of times before. As soon as Tracy mentioned that Martin never listens to her, emotions began to rise in both of them. Tracy felt alone and hurt; Martin felt attacked and got defensive because of her words. For both of them, they automatically and unconsciously picked up on the external stimuli and began to put themselves into a state of high alert – a stress reaction.

This reaction occurs in the area of the brain known as the amygdala, which is thought to be responsible for feelings and emotions, survival instincts, and memory formation. Sometimes it is referred to as the "fight-flight-freeze response center" because the body engages immediately in a "fight, flight, or freeze" response. It is prepared for action. It prepared Martin and Tracy as their bodies prepared to fight back in response to the wrongs perpetrated against them. Blood flow increases all over the body, causing the heart rate to escalate. Fists and teeth might clench, muscles often tense, and one might even break a sweat. Blood flow over the left eye to the frontal lobe increases immediately as the left frontal lobe is the part of the brain that helps us sort things out; this is the part that prevents Martin and Tracy from doing or saying things they would later regret. It is the part of the brain associated with reason.

Feelings of defensiveness, anger, frustration, and hurt are all felt most vigorously in their first several seconds of impact; then they subside. This is why your mom may have told you, "If you're angry, count to 10 first, then respond." In those 10 seconds, the emotion is likely to subside significantly, unless you intently dwell on the problem or offense.

Metacommunication

It's important to think about *what* you are thinking about. It's also important to evaluate what and how you are communicating about your thoughts.

Metacommunication, like metacognition, means being aware of the words you use, as well as tone of voice, attitude, body posture, and facial expression. Each one communicates a message.

This is illustrated in the frequent misunderstandings perpetuated by emails and text messages which can be entirely misunderstood. For example, Marcy sends a quick text message to Jack telling him she is disappointed that he cannot make it for their dinner appointment because he has to work late. Jack, having been brought up in a family culture where shame was pervasive, feels shame from the word "disappointed." Upset that Marcy challenges his intentions, Jack feels attacked and becomes defensive, as indicated by a curt reply justifying the importance of why he needs to stay to "work hard" and "support the family." Offended that he is overly sensitive, an argument ensues. They finally resolved their conflict the next morning. Marcy explained that she was not attacking Jack, but was playfully expressing disappointment because she was going to miss going to a favorite old restaurant where they had their third date. However, Jack could not see her spirited smirk or her wink of the eye when she sent the first text.

Metacommunication and its accompanying cues place a context around words. Questions like: How will the individual interpret this thought? Am I communicating this the right way? Are they truly getting the message I want them to get? Do I have the right attitude? Am I too intense? These questions, when internally processed, can help make the message easier to interpret, understand, and accept.

When you are not clear on what is being communicated, whether verbally or non-verbally, all kinds of chaos can ensue. When in doubt, check it out! A puzzled or startled eyebrow can look angry to someone who is easily defensive. Ask if you are unsure why the eyebrow was raised. Don't assume. Tone can be easily misinterpreted. Rather than assuming the worst about body posture or facial expression, ask!

Even in an intense argument, a question can take you in another direction. We can choose to respond logically and intentionally, or we can react impulsively. An appropriately placed and carefully thought-out question can force one to think about what one is thinking or how the thought is being communicated. In those moments, we actually have to think about what we want to *say* and what we want to *know*. If we think about responding to a situation with a question rather than instinctively reacting, we have already taken the conversation and the accompanying thought processes to a higher level, a level beyond primal childlike thinking.

A question that takes us into metacognition can take our focus off our emotional offense and onward to analyze *why* we respond emotionally. At a physiological level, the body will direct more blood to the frontal lobe. The effect

Martin and Tracy felt as they began to think differently is a reduced "emotional" response – less heart pounding, less bodily tension. Intrinsically, they can start thinking rationally due to a question or challenge that interrupts their normal responses. They feel more in control.

In the intensity of disagreement, at the depths of emotion – feeling wronged, hurt, or defensive – one must extricate from all these feelings, words, and swirling thoughts in order to attain a higher place. Questions to ask yourself might include, "What do I need to know? What will bring clarity?" Everyone has the ability to move from an emotional response to a thoughtful response balanced by reason. When we engage these questions and train ourselves to evaluate our feelings, we decide what we want from this encounter. "How could I better understand to bring resolution, fairness, or truth?"

Although the emotions remain present, an opportunity arises for understanding your feelings in those moments of metacognition. You take control of yourself. You see beyond your anger and hurt, and the walls you put up come down. You begin to understand *why* you want to lash out. You learn to think more clearly in order to ask questions. This is the backdrop of healthier conversations and, ultimately, better relationships. When you do this, you have now set the stage to take the entire conversation into a place of metacognition where other participants in the conversation begin to think about their thoughts and feelings as well. With one simple question, we remove the focus from escalating conflicts to engaging in rational, civil discussion.

In times of conflict, reacting is often the problem. *Not* thinking about what we are thinking about (metacognition) or not thinking about *what* or *how* we are communicating (metacommunication) means we are just reacting. You might remember a time you said something mean or negative and immediately realized what you said was hurtful and you wish you could take it back. Unfortunately, words are like toothpaste: once squeezed out, there is no way you can get the toothpaste back in the tube again.

Metacognitive and metacommunication activities lead us away from regrettable, painful words we sometimes hurl during intense conflicts. Someone needs to rise above the situation in these moments of intensely uncontrollable feelings. Somebody needs to consider what is being said and what is desired in the long term. What do I want to communicate? How can this relationship improve? How can I better understand why I feel such intense feelings in this moment?

For example, imagine someone addressing you in an agitated, irritated voice saying, "Do you even have the capacity to understand beyond the thinking of a five-year-old?" Then, further imagine becoming annoyed with how you were addressed. Your non-verbal appearance might have you standing with your arms crossed, a scowl on your face, eyes squinted, and lips pursed. You might yell, "Only if I have to talk to a moron like you?"

If you want to be hurtful or to engage in a fight, you will have succeeded. However, if you want to move to a better level of communication, you need to go through a series of questions in your mind before you react. For example:

- Is she accusing me of being immature, or is she just angry about something that I am not sure of?
- Is she hurt?
- What has hurt her so badly that she ends up hurting others?
- Do I want to respond defensively and fight back?
- Is there a better way to communicate right now, or should I let her cool down?
- How can I care for her when she feels upset?

Coming up with a list of questions under stressful conditions, such as a verbal assault, takes practice, but is achievable. All of these questions could pass through one's conscious thought processes in five or six seconds. Processing them for a moment is a significant step in moving ahead with metacognition and metacommunication. Many times, the urgent response is the worst response. Sometimes the best response is to take a timeout to think.

Imagine if you said to your spouse, "Can I have some time to think about what you have said?" This response conveys their importance and that what they have said, even in anger, is important enough for you to think about. It also conveys that you will reconvene to talk further about the issues that were brought up. Metacognitive processing should be the goal, where thinking leads to a process and lifestyle of metacommunication.

Neural pathways

The human brain contains 200-300 billion neurons. Mapping out the highway system within the brain would reveal a highly complex intermingling of roadways, highways, byways, and paths crisscrossing inside the skull, giving numerous instructions to the rest of the body. This magnificent map incessantly lights up with electrical impulses and wiring that attaches to the central nervous system and runs the body with top-down management.

A "neural pathway" is the scientific way of describing a "brain rut" – a roadway formed from repeated thinking. The brain does not discriminate between right or wrong thinking as it establishes a pathway. The more a route is travelled, the more the pathway simply becomes an entrenched passageway. These pathways in the brain form when a certain behavior and the corresponding way of thinking occur again and again.

The term "neural pathway" is an appropriate label for how the mind forms a habitual route of neurological progression. It is a path of least resistance because the behavior is repetitive and routine. It is a "habit" for lack of a better word.

We are creatures of habit. These neural pathways cannot be reduced merely to a pattern of animal behavior like a Pavlovian dog or a random, inexplicable instinct. The mind, neurologically and physiologically speaking, displays tendencies similar to any electronic circuit following the path of least resistance.

Once we repeat a particular progression of thoughts, the mind continues firing that same electrical circuit when we go down that path again. Therefore, habits can be hard to break.

Picture Sam, a four-year-old boy, getting ketchup all over his new white t-shirt at a backyard birthday party. When his mom picks him up from the party, she jokingly inquires in front of two of his friends and a little girl he likes and says, "Sam, what is that you're wearing?" pointing at the ketchup stain. He feels embarrassed. He dreams about it several times that week.

Eleven-year-old Sam, hoping for any kind of attention, ventures out to wear a comical "I'm with Stupid" t-shirt and red suspenders to school. The same girl, he still likes, asks, "What is that you're wearing?" She and three other girls giggle and run away. He's embarrassed again. He remembers the same cycle of thoughts from his earlier life's humiliation and rehearses the event frequently throughout the following months. Each time he sees one of those girls at his junior high school he rolls his eyes and thinks, "I'm such a loser." He suffers other wardrobe embarrassments over the next several years, making them out to be much worse than they are. It has become a recurring sore spot for Sam.

On his honeymoon, Sam puts on a Hawaiian shirt to wear to the dining room at their vacation resort. His wife merely glances at the shirt with a loving look in her eyes and smiles, but the innocence of her gaze is misunderstood. He misinterprets her smile as mockery and judgmental disdain. His thoughts take him down the path of inferiority and shame, leading to more self-loathing. Reacting defensively, he snaps at his new bride with a sarcastic, "Oh? And what right do you have to call yourself the fashion police?" He leaves, slamming the hotel room door behind him.

She stands wounded and alone in the hotel room thinking, "What just happened? What is his problem? I didn't even say a word! Why is he so angry that he would storm out of the room? What have I gotten myself into?"

Sam is stuck in a neural rut – a familiar experience. In these sensitive conditioned moments, his brain fires the neurons found along that familiar memory, causing him to recall the same negative feelings. His amygdala has kicked into high gear, feeling the old pain that cause his emotions to swell and his defenses to rise up. The problem is that Sam's brain has established a neural pathway triggered by anyone commenting about or even glancing at what he is wearing. He is now incredibly defensive and sensitive about anything having to do with any issue surrounding potential fashion embarrassment. This first lovers spat is triggered by a negative neural pathway around the issue of apparel which, in his mind, is associated with hurt, pain, embarrassment, and shame. Anytime the thought of his clothing comes up for him, he puts up defensive walls.

Wisdom of Allport

If Sam behaved as a young child, he would be in big trouble relationally. He would perhaps say silly immature things without a clue as to why he was behaving in such a manner. As adults, we have the power to change. We do not have to be trapped permanently in a cycle of negativity. We can think about our thoughts and feelings and arrest this process.

Regardless of how deeply the pathway is formed, we are human beings that can develop beyond immature, childlike thinking. Decades ago, sociologist and psychologist Gordon Allport realized the incredible potential we all have to change and grow and consequently called us not just human beings, but "human becomings." He said, "Personality is less a finished product than a transitive process. While it has some stable features, it is at the same time continually undergoing change."[1] However difficult, we can change entire patterns of communication. Regardless of how entrenched our behavior may have become in our lives, it is *not* too late to change.

Allport was a proponent of self-awareness as a significant component in the journey of "becoming." Becoming aware of our ruts and blind spots is difficult because they are so entrenched. To discern my blind spots and to progress, I must interrupt my thinking, or get someone to interrupt my thought process. I believe strategic questions are one of our greatest tools to exposing roadblocks ingrained in our neural pathways. Awareness of our ruts and blind spots connects neural pathways.

There are few things that can point out well-established thinking patterns like questions can. Questions help me become aware of my ruts. It might be that the way I think is not healthy or appropriate or perhaps it does not even fit my circumstances. When I keep hitting the same wall, perhaps it is not the wall, but rather me that is the problem. My thinking may be the problem! Walt Kelly, in his famous Pogo cartoon strip (1972), says it best: "We have met the enemy and he is us!"

Neural plasticity

Years ago, neurologists thought the mind was primarily formed during the early childhood and then remained constant for life. Although early childhood years are, indeed, profoundly formative, recent science has taught us about the importance of "neural plasticity." Where the mind was once thought to be inflexible, we now understand it to be open to change, or "plastic" in how we process emotion, trauma, injury, environment, behavior, and thinking patterns in general. Eventually, our minds can be retrained.

As we consider this and become increasingly aware of not just our thoughts and emotions, but the more complex way we think about how we manage those thoughts and emotions, there is actually greater opportunity and ability to change what and how we think. Again, there is a strong link between asking the right kinds of questions and neural plasticity. When we help others think about their thoughts and feelings, or when others ask us questions to cause us to think about our thoughts and feelings, our minds become increasingly malleable. Neurological evidence proves this to be the case.

When you find yourself in relational difficulty, ask yourself, "What are my thoughts here that might be hurting or limiting this relationship again? Am I willing to make some genuine changes? Am I willing to look at things differently?" In doing so, you are becoming aware of your relational neural pathways and related thoughts. At this point you can decide if you want to change those thoughts and their patterns.

Fran and Clay are a couple I journeyed with for a while. Clay struggled with rejection issues that required time to discuss and overcome. The self-pity "loop" has played continually in Clay's mind for years.

When conflict arises between Clay and Fran, he often battles the "poor me" thoughts rooted in his feeling of rejection. He carries the belief that he is not good enough. When something Fran says triggers feelings of rejection, he withdraws into defensiveness, or what is referred to as "stonewalling." While his feelings are valid, Clay and Fran now see and manage them. In this circumstance, one of their best tools is this short question: "Did Fran actually say 'You're not good enough?'" No! Fran never said that. Clay *is* good enough. The playing field became leveled. There is no superior partner denigrating a subordinate. They are now two equal partners working towards a solution. The old neural pathway based on hurt and rejection has been identified, and a new way of thinking is now instituted. One question turns the spiraling conversation around.

After repeatedly identifying these unwanted feelings, Clay and Fran are more successfully relating. Clay now *gets* it. He no longer believes he is inferior; it is merely a feeling that pops up whenever Fran makes a statement that triggers a negative memory. Clay immediately questions his reaction and implements the tools he used to retrain his brain: self-awareness, challenging emotions, and repetition of new thoughts.

I recently watched a video about a bicycle with counter steering that demonstrates how the mind can be retrained. When you turn the bike to the left, the front wheel turns to the right, and vice versa. Videos of this experience are available online. You might think that merely knowing the principle of a counter-steering bike would allow you to master it, but mental understanding alone renders it literally impossible. Because a bicycle is in a perpetual state of imbalance, there are too many micro adjustments your body has learned to keep the bicycle in balance that you can't compensate for the new ones. For example, as you push off to start riding, you may feel the momentum nudging you slightly to the right. To compensate, you might adjust by turning the steering ever so slightly to the left; however, just a slight pull to right is enough to stop all forward progress because, in your mind, you have known for years that when your imbalance is pulling you right you should adjust by slightly turning to the left. With a counter-steering bicycle, this small correction causes you to become unbalanced, ending the ride in a few seconds.

There is a significant difference between knowing the simple concept of counter steering and actually implementing it into a new riding style. In the video, the individual with the counter steering bicycle spent eight months of frequent riding to learn this new riding skill. It took his brain eight months to retrain. Once he mastered the art of riding a counter-steering bike, he tried riding a regular bike. It took him several minutes to relearn the original skill.

Again, the mind can be retrained. The neural components show an incredible capacity for plasticity, for retraining, but it takes incredible levels of repetition and then subsequent reinforcement to relearn old behaviors deeply recessed in neural pathways. Therefore, if you find yourself in the middle of difficult relationship issues, constant marriage conflicts, or interpersonal tensions, they can be resolved. Never give up hope. Typically, it takes at least three months and sometimes more to retrain the brain – depending on the effort given – to learn a whole new way of thinking. Constant reinforcement leads to success.

Limbic system: Effects of stress

When you hear a crash in the night, the limbic system moves into high gear to wake you. Your entire body rushes as the limbic system reacts: your heart pounds, adrenaline flows, blood pressure increases, oxygen-rich blood readies your brain and muscles, and all your senses sharpen. As with an emotional surge, you freeze, or become ready to fight or flee. Your body remains ready until your mind tells you that the danger has passed. If the dangerous situation is not resolved, or if emotions keep running high, stress will compromise your wellbeing. While your emotions rule the day, your ability to think long-term rational thoughts are diminished. You may seem to be sharper in your thoughts, but mostly in the kind of thinking that is impulsive, helping you to make quick decisions based on self-preservation. Momentarily gone are level-headed, long-term, community-based thinking that sustains relationships and workplace harmony. As mentioned earlier, those thoughts occur in the left side of the frontal lobe of your brain.

In recent years, we have begun to better understand the effects of high-level stress and other negative emotions on the body and brain. We also know that aging increases the negative effect of this stress and other negative emotions. Perpetual high levels of sustained stress significantly impede the positive effects at the blood-brain barrier (BBB), a barrier designed to protect the brain from potential harm caused by disorders in the body such as infections, hormonal imbalance, or cancer. Sustained stress depletes the replenishing process that is supposed to occur after the crisis has passed. Our body remains fixated on freezing, fighting, or fleeing. The necessary recovery to our body and to our brain is obstructed by our inability to de-escalate and think rationally and calmly. In essence, when we do not manage stress well, when we experience intense emotions or choose to hold on to negative feelings, we simply do not process thoughts well. If you do not deal with feelings, you cannot deal with facts effectively.

Risk/loss aversion

Utility Theory is an area of consideration that has volumes of literature surrounding it. However, we will only glance at it briefly as it applies to the scientific side of questions.

Daniel Kahneman, a world-renowned psychologist from Princeton University, has published extensively on human rationality. His work especially pertains to economics. He studied and co-published with the late Amos Tversky, a Stanford behavioral economist. Their Prospect Theory, a component of behavioral economic theory, is a study of how people make decisions to spend money. Their initial paper on Behavior Economic Theory, written in 1979, is considered to be a pioneer discussion on that topic challenging the traditional understanding of Utility Theory. Risk, which has been studied by neurologists for decades, causes significant neurological responses in the brain, including discomfort in making changes, fear, and vigilance. They determined that the pain of losing is about double the pleasure of winning. This pain forms an enduring mental habit to avoid everything related to loss. This aversion to loss can become a dysfunctional motivation shaping behavior that causes one to act foolishly.

The brain has a mechanism that reacts to risk. Our natural tendency is to move towards minimizing loss and maximizing wins. Gambling is a great example. Although classified as entertainment, it can become unhealthy to the point of addiction. Some visiting a casino might consider it as entertaining. Some do not care if they blow a couple hundred dollars during such a visit. They might find it exhilarating to feel the adrenaline rush associated with having $100 riding on a single bet that offers a 20% chance of winning $300.

Some people cross a line when the part of the brain that deals with risk responds neither quickly nor at all. Someone in trouble thinks, "The only way I can get my money back is to play more." Rational thinking would be, "I can leave the casino, go back to work, save money, and replenish my savings account." The ability to evaluate risk is neurologically, psychologically, and behaviorally innate within us.

Risk aversion, also called "loss aversion," is the psychological function in the brain that helps us minimize or avoid loss or risk. Several areas of the brain are involved, including the orbitofrontal cortex which is the area of the brain associated with regret and has been shown to be active during risk-averse behavior. It is a part of healthy neurological activity that keeps us away from the edge of cliffs and tells us to avoid bears and cougars in the wild. Under normal circumstances, this part of the brain acts to remind us of the negative emotions associated with loss, pain, and grief; it tells us not to bet anything, or to not risk more than our reasonable limit. If your risk aversion level is too low, you will be filled with regret after a trip to Las Vegas. Generally speaking, with the risk aversion parts of our brain, the anticipation of loss or previous experiences of loss make way for activation in parts of the brain that are associated with negative emotions – the amygdala and the anterior insula. Neurologists have tracked brain-imaging data to help people understand and make better, more informed decisions that help them succeed beyond what their instincts might be telling them.

Predictor neurons

Previously, I stated that neural pathways are repeated ways of thought, pathways or ruts that get worn or entrenched from repeated and frequent use. Neurons build memories and this benefits future behaviors. The benefit can be for a positive or negative purpose. These memories help us to anticipate situations so we can make better choices. Sometimes we may even ignore these feelings of anticipation. For example, we now have photo radar at various intersections in my community. After receiving a few expensive tickets, I now anticipate and adjust my speed when I am approaching one of these intersections. If I forget because of thinking about something else, I will inadvertently collect another speeding ticket.

As a profoundly complex mechanism, the brain reacts to risk and endeavors to protect us from dangerous extremes. However, we can override those brain messages and make adjustments, even to the point of making things worse. Sometimes we override protection messages. Eventually, evidence proves those decisions to be unhealthy. In such cases, we hastily overcompensate. Fear often drives this overcompensation. For example, the individual who loses money gambling may believe the only way they can recover their money is to put more money on the game that took it away. As a result of a fear of loss, the individual might think, "I'm down $200 and the only way I can get my money back is to have a string of luck at the roulette table!" That thinking, needless to say, can rapidly result in financial ruin. Instead, if we logically evaluate the risk, loss can be minimized or avoided. Loss aversion is all about avoiding the loss, especially the ruinous and debilitating loss that far outweighs the entertainment value or the thrill of a Vegas weekend. Avoiding more loss means the individual has to stop and consider what is the best way to stop losing.

An example of this overcompensation in relationships because of feared loss is a husband who, out of fear of losing his wife, listens only in an effort to show his wife that he is engaged, but talks more to prove he is a better listener. Fear inspires him to prove he can engage. Fear prevents him from hearing what his wife has told him she needs. He falsely believes engaging in conversation proves he listens. For his wife, engaging means to listen, unless asked to speak.

In communication, because we often expect results from each other, we force the outcomes. The partner, for example, who wants affirmation, complains in a manner that presents as insecure which may elicit a flattering comment that eliminates the complaint. If the complaining spouse anticipates a positive comment, and gets it, they will feel content and not disappointed. However, if the spouse doesn't get the expected compliment from their mate, they may feel disappointed, push harder, keep complaining, and just create more of a relational problem. Tragically, these cycles are all based on reactionary rhythms of insecurity, a fear of loss. Fear-based predictor neurons can cause us to alienate others, eventually hurting the relationship.

Reframing

We often frame decisions in terms of loss aversion. How we frame a situation in our minds strongly affects how we spend our money. In his book *The Decisive Moment*, Jonah Lehrer tells a group of people the story of an impoverished child in Africa. The specific story and details about her clothing, her food and water situation, and her life prospects are told to a number of people who, in response, give an average of $2.50 per person to the associated charity. Another group of people are told about the general statistics in her country, the millions who are affected, and the atrocious toll taken on human life in that region. Those people also respond with generosity, but only half the amount that the other group did. How we frame numbers and statistics versus how we frame the story of one sad little girl are worlds apart. Similarly, there's a significant difference in how we frame losing a specific amount or winning less. We make decisions based on how we frame or view the situation, either as a loss or as a potential smaller win.

When potential losses are studied with an MRI machine, specific parts of the brain are shown to respond and help us make decisions. When brains are viewed while considering the prospect of losing money, the amygdala is excited; this brings on negative feelings because people hate to lose money. The brain is sending that message.[2] The surprising part of the study was that the subjects who appeared more "logical" still had almost exactly the same amount of negative emotion in the amygdala, *but* they had simultaneous activity in the prefrontal cortex that was the best indicator as to whether or not they would take a risk.

At the end of the day, it comes down to this simple fact: you cannot always trust your emotions, but you can manage them. How can you better manage your emotions? By simply tuning in to and focusing on what you are thinking. Further, the best way to think about your thinking is by asking yourself questions: "Why am I feeling this way?" "What are the thoughts that are producing these feelings?" "Am I afraid of losing money? Or this relationship?" "Why am I so afraid of losing money?" "Why am I so afraid of losing this relationship?" "Why am I not being true to my own emotions in this fight?" "Why do I want to talk right now instead of listen?"

There is neurological proof to all of this. I do not have to be in the same argument for years on end with my spouse. I am not a victim of "This is how I am!" or "That is how my spouse is!" and "We will never change." I can change. We can change. It starts with my thinking. I can think about my thoughts and my feelings. I can stop the emotional rollercoaster of the same repeated escalating conflict. I can change my thinking. I can also change what I am thinking and how I am communicating my thoughts. I can ask myself the necessary questions to stop the argument even before it happens.

From risk-aversion to crisis-aversion

I have repeatedly seen relationship crisis coming to a head in my office. In those intense moments, I have seen how one spouse has an intrinsic need to know. They need to know the details. They need to know answers to questions that can sometimes do more harm than good. "Do you still love me? I need to know right this moment." They are afraid that if they do not know right now, the relationship is over. On the contrary, not knowing and not clearly defining the messages of an intensely active and excited amygdala during an intensely heated conflict is definitely best.

The fear at these points of crisis and the demand for an immediate decision is innate. We are not sure exactly why. It is somehow tied into loss aversion, how the situation is being framed at that moment. Once again, however, there is a dynamic cognitive possibility. If you are aware of the fear – rational or irrational fear – you can escape the fear. Very few things are so critical that they need to be solved in the moment. If we can move into a different level of metacognitive thinking where we get away from the emotion of fear, we can make more logical, effective decisions. Questions have the ability to neurologically move us from overwhelmingly intense emotion into a place of rational cognitive clarity. We take the emotion out of the crisis when we make statements or ask questions such as, "We're not going to solve this today, are we? Let's talk more next week. We're making progress. There is hope." We can actually think more clearly and, ultimately, change and grow.

When people feel like they are falling apart, they feel like they need an appointment to talk about their concerns immediately. In the end, they find a way to be able to wait. There is hope that something is going to happen which will bring a lot of encouragement. An appointment has been made. They are ok to wait.

Reacting defensively: A manifestation of fear

Allie and Dean perpetually got on each other's nerves. There was no doubt that they loved each other, but in conflict situations, Allie snapped at Dean, though mostly in a sarcastic fashion. She showed a sharp tongue when she was angry and she had the ability to rip Dean apart and push his buttons with a remarkable accuracy of words. One short, cutting sentence could reduce Dean to feeling like a fool. Usually that sentence included degrading Dean, which reminded him of his previous girlfriends long before he and Allie got married.

When Dean was defensive, this typically calm, cool, collected guy would transform into an emotional, confused, angry, flying-off-the-handle person. In response to Allie's action, Dean got highly defensive and lashed back at her, feeling he had to defend his past, his current shortcomings, his mistakes, and his words. It quickly escalated into a repetitive conflict where very little was ever resolved. As soon as Dean was accused or cornered, his defensive posture limited his way of seeing things. Dean did not know that his adrenal glands were releasing hormones that clouded his judgment. He was fighting a battle he could not win on a neurological level.

Dean was headed for another escalating defensive reaction and subsequent clash with Allie. I could see his blood start to boil. He clenched his jaw and fists, pursed his lips, and furrowed his brow. Essentially, he had taken a "hit" and he was angry with Allie. Allie herself was angry and hurt and mean with the short bursts of bitterness that she had just shot at Dean. As Dean took a deep breath to push back with his own hurt and defensive denunciations, I stepped in.

"Just a minute, Allie," I said. "That was quite a nasty comment you just threw out at Dean. Dean, what did you just hear? What is Allie so terribly upset about that she would say such a thing? I know you guys fight, but I believe that you really love each other." They both dropped their gaze and sheepishly responded, "Yeah, sure…"

"Dean," I continued, "what is Allie actually saying here? What does she actually need from you? Have we not been over this before? Can you explain your defensive reaction?"

Dean was doing everything in his power to think about his thinking. Finally, he managed, "Uh, yeah. I'm sorry. I am being defensive. Allie, you just want to feel like you can trust me. I didn't love those other girls. I chose you. I picked you. It wasn't even close. You are the one for me."

You could see Allie's shoulders physically drop, her angry forehead relax, her clenched mouth drop into a sad frown. She put down her proverbial gun and laid aside her protective shield and said, "Thanks. I needed that." From there, we had a real conversation working towards solutions; the defensive backlash had lost its place. Dean was thinking clearly. He broke the cycle of hostility and meanness. His soft answer turned wrath away.

Retrain your brain

Firefighters and police have a system to handle dangerous situations. Respectively, they do not think about the all-consuming inferno in front of them or the gun the perpetrator is pointing in their direction. Otherwise, natural response would tell them to shut down, avoid the situation, and run away. However, these highly skilled professionals have developed habits of making instantaneous life-saving decisions based on proven and learned action plans. Again, the first and normal response is to run from danger unless you are conditioned or self-conditioned to think of a new way to deal with life-threatening danger.

How do they do it? Practice, practice, practice. By rehearsing different scenarios hundreds of times, these first-responders learn to retrain the mind. They are challenged in the classroom to question their normal fears. These questions help to deconstruct the usual thought pattern of running away; questions retrain their minds. As they learn new procedures and strategies, then repetitively rehearse the new steps, they learn new behaviors. In doing so, they create neural plasticity which magnifies, growing bigger than the initial fear response.

Trained speakers and communicators do the same when they learn to look beyond the crowd, beyond their fears of public speaking. They eventually look forward to those opportunities to speak to large audiences and, it seems, the bigger the better. These professionals who are trained to think differently may get excited riding to a call. They might think about the opportunity to help others or even to save lives. They might just be reacting to the adrenaline rush. They have retrained their brain to respond differently.

Whether it is a conflict or an external crisis, our adrenals secrete more cortisol (the crisis hormone) under stress; this affects our bodies in many ways including the hippocampus which diminishes our ability to process clearly and rationally. However, if you can practice managing a crisis similarly to a police officer or fire fighter, you can change the learned behaviors of fear to respond differently, even talking to your boss about a raise, or talking to that belligerent co-worker no one can get along with. Most importantly, you can stop the cycle of conflict, pain, or dysfunction in your personal life or marriage.

Chapter 7

Defense mechanisms: How emotions can create problems when processing information during communication

> "If thou art pained by any external thing, it is not this thing that disturbs thee, but thy own judgement about it. And it is in thy power to wipe out this judgement now."
> – Marcus Aurelius[3]

Emotions profoundly affect communication, both positively and negatively. Accordingly, we need to focus on the dynamic of emotion and precisely how it affects dialogue.

Great barriers

The Great Barrier Reef runs for some 2,300 kilometers off the coast of Queensland, Australia. It runs parallel to the coast, creating a barrier between the deep waters beyond the continental shelf and the shoreline. The reef acts as a barrier to the huge ocean swells, thus protecting the continental shelf. This huge barrier forms the largest naturally occurring organism on our planet and is visible from outer space.

Human beings also have ways of protecting themselves. We put up mental and emotional barriers, sometimes consciously, sometimes unconsciously. These barriers protect us from getting hurt, looking foolish, feeling negative emotions, or having to process the ramifications of difficult situations and circumstances. Such barriers, called defense mechanisms, serve a purpose, especially through difficult times. However, they also can cause severe limitations in how we function. For example, a thick brick wall around your property might keep out intruders and provide a lovely place for planted vines to grow and sprawl. However, the same wall might block out needed sunlight, causing your grass or flowers to fade. If the brick wall is too high, you may never get to know your neighbors. In other words, what is meant to keep you safe can ultimately become a barrier to growth and socialization; both the brick wall example and the defense mechanisms in your life. Excessive defensiveness creates a barrier that robs you of the benefits of relationship.

Assumptions and half truths

One barrier in communication comes from assumptions and half-truths. We all are susceptible to falsely assume that we know the true facts about a matter. But in assuming rather than communicating clearly, we cannot receive the full picture, or the whole truth. When I am offended, I may blame others. Or, I can evaluate what may be a misinterpretation of the situation and then determine if I myself have made any false assumptions.

Many research papers have explored how people interpret experiences. One thing that keeps coming up is that we all tend to not see things as accurately as we think we do. For example, there is a tendency to think we have done better or worse at something than what is actually true. Or, we sometimes think the best or the worst of ourselves, or others.

Emotions and communication

Of course, emotions can complicate conversation. Emotions can distort the simple facts, thoughts, and ideas we try to convey, causing us to communicate something drastically different *and* to hear something totally contrary to what is being said. Emotions put a very unique twist on what I thought I said and what I thought I heard. Facts, thoughts, and ideas are usually straight forward before they are conveyed. However, when feelings surface, they alter the interpretation of facts. Add the nonverbal cues of tone, body language, gestures, and intonation, and simple communication quickly gets complicated. Remember this sentiment: "It's not what you said, but *how* you said it." For example, if someone states, "Come here," with a frown, clenched teeth and fists, you are likely to stay away from them rather than move forward. However, those same two words accompanied by a smile increase your likelihood of moving towards the requester.

Everyone sees things a little differently – perhaps vastly differently. Depending on your history, experiences, and background, you see, hear, and interpret information through the complicated filter of your mind, thereby producing related emotions. We need to be aware of the emotional barriers that can separate us as we attempt to communicate.

Defense mechanisms

Sigmund Freud was the founder of psychoanalysis. This neurological pioneer was a huge proponent of identifying and explaining the naturally occurring barriers, which he labelled as "defense mechanisms" (DM). Freud may have been the first to identify DMs, but he was not the only one to study them. The study of DMs developed significantly throughout the last century.

DMs are simply coping strategies, concepts, or beliefs that we use to defend ourselves. Usually, we use these subtle tendencies to protect ourselves. However, DMs often manifest without our awareness of them. While their goal may be to protect us, they may unconsciously keep others at arm's length. For a relationship to be healthy, it is important to expose the DMs. Once exposed, these barriers can be addressed and resolved through strategic means. This often results in improved communication and relationships.

There are other barriers to our relationships that also undermine friendships such as fear, anger, and shame. They will be discussed in the next chapter. However, let's first identify and describe the more commonly used DMs.

Sorting through DMs often feels like untangling a web before we can get to the facts that are at the heart of the issue. At the end of the day, we must improve communication. Questions help us sort through and discern what is a smoke screen, an actual root issue, or a fact.

Denial

Denial is the most recognized DM. Denial causes resistance against accepting reality. Denial is a euphemism for lying to yourself. Denial becomes complex when you believe your own lie vividly; you become so convinced you tell others. Such a far-reaching deception hurts or even drives relationships down to a whole new low. Alcoholics Anonymous teaches a lot about denial and the importance of confronting it.

Men in a midlife crisis are a good example. Their denial mechanism protects them from dealing with the reality of getting older which makes them feel insulated by their negative feelings toward aging. Those who go too far with their age delusion ignore the obvious truth, especially concerning health, and other areas of personal wholeness.

Or, imagine a young teenager, Brandon, getting dumped by his girlfriend. She said, "It's over. Do *not* call me again." If he thinks, "She doesn't mean it, it will all be okay tomorrow, she just needs to sleep on it," then he is not acknowledging the reality of the situation. He is in denial of the relationship's demise.

Rationalization

Rationalization is almost as commonly known as denial among DMs. To rationalize means to justify, make excuses for, or explain-away one's behavior.

Perhaps you have heard a story like Brandon's, a heart-broken teenage boy recently dumped by his girlfriend, who rationalizes by saying, "It's okay, I never really liked her that much anyways." Of course, he was absolutely crazy about her, but if he can explain away the heartbreak as being of little consequence, he protects himself by minimizing his hurt feelings.

In reality, if Brandon does not fully identify and cope with his negative feelings, he could stunt his emotional health and growth. This could cause him to implement other DMs, leaving him to remain at a shallow emotional level and to never develop the ability to communicate his feelings. The DM might serve him well to get through the day, to be able to rationalize, to save face, and to look cool with his friends. However, Brandon needs to unpack the deep hurt and rejection with a counsellor or trusted friend sooner rather than later.

Repression

Repressed emotions, especially the most painful memories, can be blocked entirely from memory. The detrimental results of those events will remain – the shame, self-doubt, low confidence level – with the root of the problem never resolved.

Imagine Brandon not just denying or rationalizing, but repressing his feelings. He unknowingly pushes them below the surface, totally repressing them. When he senses rejection or unworthiness coming to the surface, he'll unconsciously block the thoughts and feelings completely from his mind because of the pain or uncomfortable feelings associated with such emotions.

Imagine a year later when, with the girlfriend situation repressed, Brandon meets a lovely young lady with a lot in common. He may have feelings for her, but would never consider asking her for a date. His repressed unresolved feelings of not being good enough and the fear of rejection can lead to an overarching fear of further rejection, resulting in no self-confidence. Just asking the girl for coffee is not even an option for Brandon. If asked about it, he might simply respond, "I don't know. It just doesn't make sense to ask her out," or "Why would I ask her out?" The normal thought processes of a teenager interested in another teenager becomes hijacked by a new set of irrational beliefs and feelings.

Regression

Regression is vastly different from repression. To regress is to step backwards in time when confronted with unacceptable feelings or thoughts. A few years earlier as a 7-year-old, Brandon started wetting his bed when his parents' fighting escalated. Fearing a divorce, he regressed into bed-wetting that continued for three months, even though he was potty-trained at age three without any accidents for four full years. As his parents resolved their conflicts, Brandon stopped wetting his bed.

Now, as a heart-broken teenager dumped by his girlfriend, Brandon embraced a different form of regression, remaining in bed a good part of the week after the breakup. He awoke every morning feeling lousy and feeling like he needed to sleep this off. Unable to express his hurt, it was easier to avoid the daily routine, especially school, by regressing to the sanctuary of the same childhood bed and bedroom he had known for over a decade.

Acting out

When one expresses feelings through behavior rather than verbalization, that is called acting out. Brandon was raised with the highest moral and behavioral standards, but now finds himself angry for no real reason. Friends avoid him because he is no fun to be around. He may deny feeling hurt about the breakup and may not acknowledge his anger about being rejected, but for him, all he feels is self-pity.

When the acting out turns into self-harm, the implications of this DM can be even more painful. Cutting, anorexia, bulimia, over-eating, and suicide are all manifestations of acting out which are at high statistical levels among youth. Less extreme exhibitions of acting out include poor academic performance, excessive shopping, impulse buying, bad driving habits, sarcasm, mockery, bullying, defiance, and shoplifting.

Projection

With projection, the feelings, mood, behavior, or impulses of one person are wrongly accredited to another who is not feeling, thinking, or behaving that way. When Brandon is having lunch in the school cafeteria, he may accuse his friend Aaron of being afraid of getting hurt or of not wanting to risk rejection when Aaron won't ask the girl at the next table out. Brandon could spout off any number of hurtful or degrading comments, merely a reflection of his own feelings, which could bring harm to the relationship with Aaron. Aaron finally says, "Dude! She's my cousin." Brandon presumed Aaron had feelings for the girl at the lunch table because Brandon himself had feelings for her, but was not able to admit it to himself or Aaron. Brandon lacked the courage to share his true feelings, therefore he projected his hidden feelings onto Aaron.

Reaction formation

With this unique DM, a person reacts in the opposite manner of the forbidden behavior they are trying to avoid, often with great exaggeration. For example, someone who grows up in an alcoholic home, experiencing tragic hurt and pain, often find themselves in a worse struggle because they have become addicted to alcohol and drugs. They become the extreme personification of what they said they hated and would never become. They end up creating more damage than they experienced growing up. It is a tragic but a true story of loss and pain hidden behind the veil of a destructive unconscious reaction.

Disassociation

Disassociation (also called dissociation) is a DM whereby a person's mind will not remember traumatic emotional pain. For some, disassociation is called a "gift," a gap in memory to avoid remembering the pain associated with terrible events. The classic example is the adult who was abused as a child but now has no recollection of events, seasons, or even years of their childhood.

Trish, a highly functioning, successful businesswoman, had no memories of her childhood before age eleven. She heard stories from other family members concerning sexual abuse from her uncle, now imprisoned for more than a dozen charges from as many victims, mostly relatives. She denied that anything could have happened to her, that she had somehow managed to avoid the abuse that even her own sister went through. Six years after her wedding, frustrated with her sexuality, her marriage was at a point of crisis, so she sought help.

Everything changed with Trish when she attended a professional women's retreat called "Success Begins Within." The speaker asked, "Are there any secrets, habits, or barriers in your heart keeping you from being all that you were created to be?" When the ladies took time at the end of the session to journal and reflect, her first memories of abuse surfaced. She faced the reality that she could not deal with as a little girl until she was almost 30 years old, a history she blocked from memory for 20 years. Her mind had disassociated from this abuse. She had no idea it took place until her memories returned. Thus, began a four-year journey of transparency, openness, and healing that revolutionized Trish. This life-changing narrative began with a simple question.

Compartmentalization

Compartmentalization has its roots in the cognitive dissonance that exists because of inner conflict between beliefs, emotions, ethics, or values. As these conflicting views are categorized into compartments, people can accommodate their angst and tension about what they are feeling and thinking. Ryan was a self-confessed environmentalist who pursued an engineering degree, thinking he could really make a difference. He dabbled in various career options for a few years after graduation. When he met the love of his life, Leanne, they married within eight months and had three kids over the next five years. Ryan accepted a position in the oil and gas industry helping extract oil through a process called fracking. He had actually taken part in a public protest, 15 years earlier, against the same process that he would now fully engage in.

When a close university friend asked about his change of position, he said, "Well, I have to feed the family, right?" Ryan has essentially compartmentalized his former environmental protest days as part of his youthful enthusiasm.

Undoing

Undoing entails the deconstruction of a formerly held belief, ideal, or action by acting out the opposite, to negate or compensate for previous words or actions.

Rick had been faithful to his wife for over 30 years. He ruined his perfect track record while on a business trip. The next day after arriving home, he bought his wife flowers when he came home for supper. He had not done that since they were engaged. She knew something was up. She never would have suspected his infidelity if he had not come home with flowers. Later, he admitted that he wanted to get caught. Unconsciously, he drew attention to his mistake in order to expose his error, thereby dealing with it, in hopes of repairing his struggling marriage.

Intellectualization

Intellectualization is an avoidance technique in which one journeys into reason. Painful or awkward emotions are avoided with this DM by hiding behind facts and logic.

Susan, a nurse, was sexually assaulted years ago while walking to her apartment near the hospital after work one night. She never talked about the pain or emotional scars of this event but instead invested her energy into upgrading her nursing credentials by pursuing a Master's degree. As much as possible, she centered her studies around the psychological effects of trauma on victims, the topic of her thesis. Although she knew much about the issue, she never talked about her memories and pain. She knew why she should, but it took years for her to finally share her story.

Her breakthrough moment came when she was observing a recovery group for victims. A participant asked her, "Why are you so interested in this topic?" Susan hemmed and hawed. She gave theoretical and statistical reasons, weaving an intricate story of how important it is from a research perspective to help those who have been sexually traumatized. Then, she finally admitted for the first time, "Because I was raped too." At that point, she said, the "dam burst open" and all of the feelings she had kept hidden behind a wall of intellect broke out explosively. After

75 minutes of recounting her story, she felt as though the weight of the world had lifted off her shoulders. One question dismantled her wall of intellectualization in mere seconds.

Displacement

Displacement, another Freudian DM, is the unconscious act of replacing old goals and objectives with new ones because it is believed that the old ones may result in dangerous or inappropriate outcomes. In typical Freud fashion, many of these have to do with inappropriate aggression, sexual urges, or fantasies.

Many examples of displacement in psychology textbooks use the story of the man who gets yelled at by his boss, goes home and is grouchy with his wife, who in turn is mean to the daughter who picks on her little brother by teasing him. Ultimately, in all of these examples, a little boy ends up getting mad and kicks the family pet.

Oddly enough, it only takes one person to break the cycle. It is the one who asks, "Why am I so irritable today?" or "Why are they so irritable?" Metacognition – thinking about the thinking – can put the brakes on a succession of events where one person gets upset and takes it out on another. Someone can stop the cycle if they can understand what is happening.

Sublimation

Sublimation is considered a more mature DM, whereby inappropriate impulses, temptations, or desires are transformed into more constructive, profitable, or acceptable behaviors.

Jules was an intensely angry gentleman who got into trouble with alcohol in his younger years. As an adult, he became a compulsive eater when he was angry. When we talked about healthier ways to deal with his anger, his wife suggested, "Why don't you join a hockey league?" It was also suggested he start jogging to get in shape for the hockey season. Not only did he get in shape, he found jogging really helped him calm his anger — especially the deep breathing associated with the aerobic exercise. His life improved because of a suggestion disguised as a question.

Assertiveness

Extreme communication responses range between timidity (shyness or passivity) and aggression (even anger or abrasiveness). Assertiveness is the appropriate respectful, middle ground on the communication scale. This functional DM helps introverts to be able to cope optimally. They can speak up for themselves, be heard, and express themselves in the context of relationships.

Interestingly, many of the courses that teach assertiveness, directly or under the guise of another topic, utilize deconstructionist questions to challenge the rationality of the fear of speaking up. Once again, questions make a great impact and change behaviors for the good.

Compensation

Compensation makes up for weakness in one area by being strong in a different area.

There is a recurring storyline behind numerous bodybuilders, professional fighters, boxers, and wrestlers. Many experienced some kind of bullying as a kid, motivating them to spend hundreds of hours in the gym to transform themselves into rough, tough warriors. For example, Muhammad Ali entered boxing after another boy stole his bike. The determination to prevent being bullied or taken advantage of has driven many to achieve great levels of success.

Isolation

This final DM involves the creation of a barrier between positive thoughts and feelings, and negative ones – ultimately by focusing on positive thinking and minimizing negativity with its accompanying stress. Isolation is about defending the ego, protecting self-esteem, and avoiding a discouraging negative view of oneself. In *Repression of Emotionally Tagged Memories: The Architecture of Less Complex Emotions,* Hansen coined the phrase "architecture of less complex emotions" to describe this isolation.[4]

For example, a shopkeeper robbed at knife point may appear calm, cool, and collected as she pulls out a baseball bat, telling the assailant to get out of the store immediately. Her emotions are contained while managing the situation because of her training in crisis protocol. After the robber flees, she is so shaken she cannot even dial 911. She isolated her true feelings of fear in order to make it through the stress of the foiled robbery, but when the stress response dissipates, the feelings of fear quickly rise to the surface. The true feelings emerge eventually.

Why is it important to know these DMs?

Not all DMs are bad. In times of change, conflict, and turmoil, DMs serve the purpose of helping us by giving us time and space to process. They serve as a buffer, protecting our minds and bodies until we can think through, sort out, and consciously find a way forward. When DMs become our acceptable permanent method of dealing with situations, and when we believe the lies associated with them, they become detrimental to our emotional health and relational success. Emotionally intelligent individuals can identify the preceding DMs in their own lives. When self-aware, they orchestrate action steps that avoid damaging personal well-being and surrounding relationships.

To ignore these DMs is to embrace dysfunction. Deep in our hearts lies a better version of ourselves, waiting to break out — a more honest, more whole, more complete individual who needs to stop pretending. As a more authentic and transparent person, one longs to function more fearlessly, more lovingly with others.

Self-Awareness

Sorting through one's DMs is a huge task that gets even more complex when DMs weave together. We will all benefit from a basic understanding of how DMs interact with each other. In theory, DMs follow recurring patterns as they pile up and play out – as we saw, to some degree, with Brandon. Thus, defense mechanisms follow a predictable course that can be useful in diagnosing and helping people understand themselves. If you are avoiding issues, you may need help seeing yourself in a true perspective. Do not hesitate to get professional help.

With the basic understanding about DMs that you now possess, there are three important questions you should ask yourself:

1. **What DMs do I use most frequently?** I doubt that anyone uses all 16 of the DMs listed on the preceding pages. However, self-awareness will help identify which DMs you use the most. Whichever they are, it is vital to identify your actions (especially the dysfunctional ones), label them, address them, take full responsibility for them, and be accountable to those with whom you are in relationship.

2. **When do I exhibit the DMs I employ?** Knowing what triggers dysfunctional responses and activities will help you learn how to overcome DMs. You'll set better boundaries for yourself. If necessary, you can avoid unhealthy situations until you have established these boundaries. Being aware of the triggers helps you set up a new system, a new lifestyle, a new way of navigating the forest of emotion and DMs that surround you.

• **Do I know *why*?** Where did you learn this DM? When can you first remember displaying this DM? What about your past causes you to engage in this particular DM? If you are able to identify the root or source of the pain you are trying to cope with, you will discover a way to heal that pain. Cognitive Behavioral Therapy (CBT), for example, helps you dig deeper than you would through a conversation with a trusted friend. If you cannot readily discern the root cause of an issue or dysfunctional behavior, I would encourage you to consider this approach. This could start your journey toward improved emotional health.

Chapter 8

Fear, anger, and shame

"Flowers are restful to look at. They
have neither emotions nor conflicts."
– Sigmund Freud

We use defense mechanisms to guard and protect ourselves from pain. Perhaps it is literal physical pain we are avoiding, but most times it's the pain of emotions, the ache of feelings that we are desperately trying to avoid. We go to great lengths and desperate measures to avoid dealing with these emotional struggles. In fact, I have seen hundreds of clients whose entire lives are frustrated, confused, derailed, altered, or harmed because they have emotional issues that have not been properly sorted, discussed, and repaired. They live their lives trying to compensate for their pain and hurt rather than fixing the underlying issues.

I have found that questions can lead individuals out of a maze of confusion, the downward spiral of destructive thinking that has injured and ruined years of their lives. Asking them the proper questions can radically transform their lives.

Cognitive changes and behavioral modifications do not occur overnight. If we can get to the root of the issues, deconstruct the underlying untruths and deceptions, and ask questions to change thought processes, then we can see people gradually engage in transformation that significantly improves their quality of life. The underlying issues are often related to fear, anger, and shame.

Fear

Terri presented with a deep fear of abandonment. In the initial appointment, she shared how many of the various relationships she had over the years had been impacted, mostly adversely, because of it. As a psychologist, I hear these stories often. I knew what she should do. I knew what direction she would have to go. I shared the solution.

However, at Terri's next appointment, she said, "I wasn't going come back today because you didn't hear me last week." Ironically, listening is a large part of my job. Yet, her fear caused her to judge me for not truly listening.

For the next six months I heard and explored the depths of Terri's story. Through the counselling process I asked a lot of questions in order to develop a good understanding of her story. I also wanted to ensure that Terri had the opportunity to express and reflect on her story and to make sure she was experiencing what she hoped to achieve through the counselling process. Six months later, Terri realized that she had come to the same solutions that were presented to her previously.

With her fear of abandonment, however, a quick solution was very different from the whole solution. Being heard, feeling safe, and participating emotionally required a journey of six months. This lengthy process helped Terri to build trust before she was emotionally ready to hear the solutions.

For many, fear becomes an insurmountable obstacle, creating a pessimistic mindset based on previous experiences like hurt, pain, suffering, or injury of some kind. Fear causes doubt. Some have difficulty making decisions because they fear making a mistake or missing out on something better or more important to them. Fear can also be outright debilitating, ruinous, and gripping. Fear of commitment, for example, can leave a guy like Matt single and miserable for the entirety of his life because he fears the experience of potential divorce. This fear developed in Matt's youth. When his parents yelled, Matt would get overwhelmed by the tension. Offhanded statements like, "I want a divorce," put Matt on edge. Although his parents stayed together, Matt always feared they would divorce. He became a strongly independent, perpetual bachelor who remained shallow with women he dated. Finally, he met someone he wanted to marry. Yet after a five-year engagement, he broke it off, never wanting to commit. An initial question, "What are you so afraid of?" traced his journey back decades to a point that exposed why he was so afraid. The understanding he developed changed his life.

Day-to-day fear

I find fear to be very prevalent in many of the people I meet. Few are aware of how fear impacts their lives. Anecdotally, I have found women struggle with fear even more than men.

Perhaps you think you do not have issues with fear. However, if you have ever experienced anxiety, insecurity, shyness, worry, alarm, or nervousness (which are considered the cousins of fear), then you have experienced fear in some form.

Because of fear, people establish barriers around themselves. Such walls frustrate people who are trying to communicate with them.

Breaking the cycle of fear and anger

Let me share a story of a relationship almost ruined by fear. A woman came in to my office seeking help. She had come in for appointments previously with her husband, but he would not express himself openly. She was extremely frustrated with him. Occasionally, she would contemptuously blow up at her husband. In doing so, she let off some steam, which got the building sense of pressure and frustration out of her system. More importantly, she would finally get some response from her non-communicative husband.

The cycle continued, but the frequency changed. Initially, she would blow up every eight to 10 weeks, but gradually dropped to six weeks, five and then four. I suspected the core issue in their conflict to be a fear of rejection. Neither felt safe to be angry. They were living in fear of rejection from each other. At that point, I suggested, "Why don't we ask him if he *is* angry."

"Ask him if he's angry?" she retorted. "I already *know* he's angry!"

"Let's ask," I continued. "You may know that he is angry, but you should ask the question to engage him."

Eventually she agreed and asked him if he was angry. Immediately, he said he was not. For five straight days she patiently repeated the same question once a day, wanting to know if he was angry. He finally admitted the truth: he *was* angry.

The ice was broken. She then ventured to ask a follow-up question. "What are you angry about?"

"Nothing," he replied. There was no response that day, nothing at all. With the same level of patience and perseverance, she reiterated the same question for the next four days. He continued to give no response. Finally, on the fifth day, she asked again but this time he responded: "I'm angry because you don't seem to listen to me."

The anger was part of the issue, but what was hurting this relationship even more was the fear that prevented them from finding a measure of resolution. Eventually, the husband emerged from behind his wall of fear. He saw her behavior as safe. He shared a little bit and there was no blow up. He shared a little more. Still, there was no blow up. He had finally found a safe place. Then, and only then, did he open up and honestly share how he felt. After that encounter, they would go for walks together and talk about deep, intimate things for hours on end. Not long after, he came for counselling on his own. He realized he had issues of his own he needed to work on. He opened up and dug deep into his past. From behind the barrier he had built, he could not see himself for who he really was. He believed he could never defend himself when his wife would blow up. A simple statement – "Let's ask him if he's angry" – was the key to unlocking years of tension and marital frustration. A simple question – "Are you angry?" – where the answer was already known and fairly obvious opened the door for the husband to have a safe dialogue with his wife.

The lesson from this encounter is both simple and profound. When a partner is not shooting their proverbial gun, blowing up or setting off explosions, questions can be asked in a safe environment, leading to engagement and resolution. The lady in the above situation established some boundaries and parameters and stuck to them. They paid off. Rather than blowing up, she stuck to her simple script of asking the same question and patiently waited for an honest response, no matter how long it took. A question provided the framework for an open, honest dialogue. The communication improved dramatically because they both took risks. Relationships improve as communication improves.

Anxiety

Anxiety often becomes a euphemism for fear. With both fear and anxiety, people anticipate future trouble by asking repeated "What if?" questions. Such questions are valid because anxiety, fear, worry, insecurity, nervousness, and shyness all may arise from legitimate sources.

In his book *The Fear Shift: Dominated by Fear No More*, psychologist Graham Bretherick points out two kinds of fear: negative and positive.[5]

Positive fear identifies real and imminent danger. This fear can save your life. Bretherick tells a story of when he drove through the mountains and saw smoke behind his car that he thought was an exhaust pipe emission. When he took his foot off the gas pedal, he saw smoke still coming from the rear of the car. He was no longer just worried – he was afraid. When he got out to inspect the situation, he opened the trunk and flames shot out. He was able to partly extinguish the flames with juice before a passing trucker doused the flames with a fire extinguisher. The fear he felt when he saw the smoke was positive and useful. Similarly, such fear in general helps us identify what matters most to us.

Bretherick then describes negative fear as "the fear of fear." While positive fear is helpful, negative fear is irrational and becomes debilitating. This fear is often based on negative emotions found in our memories, particularly the unhealed, unhealthy recollections of the past. For example, sometimes accident victims are terrified to get into another car after they have been in an accident. It may be perfectly safe and statistically unlikely that they will get in another accident any time soon, but they can be crippled by the fright of the negative potential.

Positive fear is your friend, one that can save your life. Negative fear is a way of thinking that needs to be challenged. Negative fear needs to be sorted through, understood, managed, and subdued. Asking the right questions of yourself or another person disentangles us from the crushing fear-based thinking that holds us back.

I believe that cognitive behavioral therapy (CBT) is a tremendous approach to help individuals get free from negative fear. The goal of CBT is to enable people to recognize their beliefs and then to challenge the dysfunctional ones. The more understanding we get, the freer we become. When anxiety and fear perpetually drive us to ask, "What if?" CBT consistently responds with the question, "So what?"

Hannah was very frustrated with her husband's response when she asked him to take out the garbage. He said he was sick of her nagging. I asked her, "What are you so concerned about with respect to the garbage?"

"If I don't ask him to take it out, it will overflow!" Hannah answered.

"Jesse," I asked, "will you take out the garbage? Have you agreed that it's your job?"

"Yeah, sure," Jesse said. "I've agreed to it, but I hate being nagged about it."

I asked Hannah, "So what if it overflows?"

Hannah said, "That's disgusting! It has to be cleaned up!"

I pushed a little more. "Whose job is it to clean up the garbage?"

Jesse immediately volunteered, "It's my job."

I asked, "So, if the garbage overflows, he will clean it up, right?"

Hannah, visibly upset, said, "But we can't have our kitchen garbage overflowing! What if somebody sees that?"

I know most people do not have overflowing garbage cans in their kitchen. However, Hannah's concern over what most people think, was a bigger issue than living at peace with Jesse. So I asked again, "So what?"

The "So what?" question ended when Hannah no longer nagged Jesse about the garbage and several other little jobs. Eventually, Hannah got over her fear of looking bad to other people. The fear created by Hannah's perfectionist tendencies was assuaged when she realized that Jesse was more consistent with taking out the garbage. In reality, it only overflowed once every two or three months. The kitchen garbage was under the sink where no one ever saw it. Further, when it did overflow,

Jesse would clean it up because that was his job. Being challenged with a "So what?" question helped Hannah get to the root of her fear that caused her to nag Jesse to the point of significantly built-up tension.

Questions challenge negative fear and anxiety. I often ask clients questions such as, "Can you help me understand the anxiety you're feeling today? So what would be the problem if that did happen today? What could you do about it?" When practiced repeatedly, this type of dialogue will change how they think. New neural pathways are created, and new habits of thinking are learned. Each of us has the ability to internalize new thought processes and begin thinking very differently.

I have observed this shift occur in many patients who were dealing with triggers to which they had substantially reacted, but now they were unbothered. They learned to talk it through by asking themselves questions such as, "What would happen if…? Can I do anything to change it? Would it help me to worry?" Moreover, when they talk about legitimate worries, they can verbalize the "What if?" questions. In doing so, they come to their own realizations about the situation: "Oh, I know how this would go. I can see where this line of thinking is going." Accordingly, they can stop themselves and self-regulate.

Settling these concerns for themselves greatly benefits individuals. Not only is there a personal advantage of moving away from suspicion, fear, anxiety, or doubt, but there is an intrapersonal advantage as they interact with others. They no longer function in a fear-based capacity, but with intentionality as they embrace opportunities to respond positively. I applaud how they wisely make progress in these areas. Rather than thinking with fear, doubt, and cynicism, they have turned toward a more positive perspective of faith, hope, and love. This allows them to believe for the best.

A significant advantage for kids occurs when we help them process fear-arousing situations. Clinically, I know from experience that kids feel much more anxious these days. It is no wonder, as adults themselves cannot figure out why they feel what they feel. Unfortunately, adults pass that sense of uncertainty down to the next generation.

Prior to the 1990s, kids were afraid of nuclear bombs, the cold war, the Nazis – events occurring on the other side of the globe. In that era, kids were taught about bomb shelters and survival techniques.

Today, the source of our fear is not across the seas. With the proliferation of media outlets, not only does the media report events that substantiate our fears, but also hundreds of blogs, websites, and 24-hour news and cable channels push notifications through smartphones that tell us the danger is everywhere. While we appreciate amber alerts and warnings, far too much negative fear pervades our society.

Assault-prevention training programs teach important concepts of safety, especially to children; however, training cannot prevent every crisis. Teaching a generation to ask questions in an anxiety-filled society reduces fear and turmoil. Whether it is "intra" (inward – I have to ask myself questions) or "ultra" (outward – I have to ask questions of the situation), our kids must learn the skills to ask questions for their own protection: "Why is that car slowing down? Why is he talking to me? If my parents have sent you, what's our password for special situations?" These questions can keep kids safe and help them function in the midst of anxious situations. Proper questions help kids anticipate dangerous situations without being fearful or bound up by anxiety.

Insecurity

The word "insecurity" is not as strong as the word "fear," but it is another expression of the same emotion. Insecurity seems even more invasive as the teeth of fear sink into our own personal space and latch on to our personality and psyche. Those who struggle with insecurity are not confident or secure in themselves. They may even dislike or hate themselves.

Heather presented an intelligent, confident, and self-assured professional, wife, mother, and friend. Her great smile and winsome personality quickly disarm anyone who approaches her. She is a person of her word, is caring, warm, and reliable in every way. But as a teenager, she believed she had some physical flaws. Her perfect smile did not come easily. She struggled with her looks, her braces, and some other perceived shortcomings that tormented her in those awkward years of adolescence. By the time she was 20, those somewhat irrational insecurities were part of the distant past, but the memories themselves did not fade. She lacked confidence, second guessed herself, and often felt withdrawn or that she was better off alone. Despite reassurances from her husband, friends, and family, she remained timid and insecure. She hesitated to meet others and avoided appointments and connections because she fundamentally did not believe in herself. She was insecure.

Heather needed help to turn her opinions around. She felt she was destined to continue those insecure feelings unless someone could help revolutionize her way of thinking. By asking her the right questions, she broke the root of the lies that had found their way deep into her belief system, which were strengthened through years of negative reinforcement. Those destructive beliefs had become part of her identity despite all the positive encouragements that had been spoken to her and about her. Questions turned this around by challenging the erroneous assumptions her entire life has been built on.

Enmeshment

Enmeshment is a term that applies to families that are too interconnected and overly concerned and involved with each other's lives to a point of dysfunction. Many times, enmeshment is linked to roots of fear — fear of loss, losing control, or some other manifestation of fear.

In acute cases, children or teenagers can feel as though the only way to escape extreme enmeshment is suicide. Children in enmeshed families feel they have no freedom to develop a sense of self or independence. Any act of independence is considered an act of rebellion. In their book *Family Therapy*, Herbert and Irene Goldenberg describe it very succinctly: "A child sneezes, his sister runs for the tissue, his mother for a thermometer, and his father starts worrying."[6] In such a family unit, the normal boundaries and rules are blurred.

Perhaps you have heard of or known an enmeshed family like this. They do almost everything together. They exhibit an unhealthy sense of attachment to each other. There is often an obvious desire or need for control. Usually, the underlying root cause of enmeshment is fear.

The Kents were such a family. They seemed to be tightly knit together. Colin and Carrie came for help and wisdom for a "huge family issue" that was causing tension. Their older child, Christine, had her grade eight year-end school trip coming up. It was going to be a double-overnighter – out of town, hotel, mall, museums, and a four-hour bus ride, a fun-filled extravaganza. This was to be a significant rite of passage for Christine. Several of the students had never been away from their parents overnight before, including Christine.

Colin and Carrie were willing to pull the other three kids out of school, get a room at the same hotel and just be there for her in case anything went wrong. Healthy fear is one thing, but this reflected a whole new level of enmeshment. The questions to ask in a situation like this are: "Do you think this is normal behavior? What if every family did this? Would there even be room at the hotel?"

For children or adolescents to grow into healthy, functional adults, parents must encourage independence. A well-supervised school trip provides a great opportunity for junior high kids to blossom in taking calculated risks by breaking away from their families for a few days. So the deeper question is, "What are you afraid of?" Follow that up with, "So what?" These questions have the uncanny ability to explore a sense of normalcy – including what is socially and age-appropriate. In the end, Christine's parents and siblings stayed home. I suspect the family worried both nights.

Fear cannot dominate our lives. Questions challenge our thinking by putting a healthy border around fear.

In another situation, I worked with a young couple in the process of breaking away from their enmeshed families. Daryl and Sarah did not know where they were in their own development as a couple, or even as individuals. For both of them, communication was a problem in their families of origin.

As I inquired about their new marriage, the accompanying problems, and potential future problems, I asked the questions: "Are there any family dynamics that you do not want to include in your marriage going forward? Are there ways that you would like to develop your marriage that would be an improvement over what you have observed in others?"

Both Daryl and Sarah decided they wanted to establish their own traditions while still maintaining good relationships with their parents and siblings. One change they agreed on, for example, was they would not attend some of the family functions which could potentially upset the rest of the family. However, in setting up healthy boundaries, Daryl and Sarah prioritized their marriage without cutting off their families. They scheduled family time with their respective parents on a regular basis because they felt they should have control over their own schedules so as to not be drawn in to other's demands. The important and redemptive point about Daryl and Sarah's stand is that the parents are now respecting their boundaries.

Boundaries need such acts of kindness to balance new lifestyle limitations. Daryl and Sarah did not ask, "How can we write off our family traditions?" but rather, "How can we set healthy boundaries and still embrace our family in a loving way?" I believe they found a proper balance. Daryl and Sarah now understand themselves better as individuals having differentiated themselves from their extended family traditions and are defining their relationship with each other more clearly and in a healthy manner.

Dr. Wilf Kent often jokes about the marriage bed, saying that after marriage you can see the families of origin in bed with the newlywed couple. He suggested that if you don't define yourselves apart from your family of origin, you are essentially bringing them to bed with you. We will bring our family of origin issues into every intimate part of the marriage if we do not intentionally and strategically define who we are now: a new couple and a new family unit. Some have been married for decades while some individuals have been married several times because they failed to delineate exactly who they are as a new couple and family. Daryl and Sarah saw the values they wanted from their families of origin. They removed what they did not want and kept what they valued. Eventually, they built a functional relationship together with extended family within mutually acceptable and beneficial parameters.

Have you wrestled through the discomfort of relationship boundaries with your parents, friends, and relatives? Or have you been bullied into accepting an uncomfortable lack of boundaries? If you dread meeting or connecting with family or friends because you feel uncomfortable or afraid, then maybe you have not sorted out your boundaries. Establishing boundaries is healthier than avoiding relationships because of fear of conflict. You do not have to be a victim.

Anger

Consider this example. You are at work and the boss checks in on how a project is going with one of your coworkers. Unfortunately, you had to deal with situations at home earlier that morning with the kids, rides, a miscommunicated appointment, and you came to work 10 minutes late. Usually you are very prompt and you have a reputation of not just being on time, but being 10-25 minutes early. When your boss asks about the project you are working on, a coworker blurts out, "Well, we'd be right on track if she could just keep up with the rest of us and get to work on time!"

You have a choice in that moment. You defensively blurt out, "Yeah, I was late today for the first time in two years, but you are *always* a few minutes late! That's the pot calling the kettle black." Is it appropriate to join the ranks of mudslingers and throw others under the bus? Usually not. Better to bite our tongues than lash out in rage. We want to appear cool and collected so we brush it off and move on believing the boss will see the immaturity and character flaws of the coworker.

A volcano under the surface?

But what is going on with us under the surface? Even if we don't show it, those kinds of sarcastic comments can annoy us. You might feel your blood pressure rise, the tension in your neck, shoulders, or back increase as you absorb the emotional stress. You might consider yourself angry, but perhaps you're a bit ticked off or one of the other words for entry-level anger: bothered, irritated, annoyed, frustrated, moody, or insulted. Call it what you want, your body was created to handle situations like this with the anger alarm system.

In his book *Healing Life's Hurts*, Bretherick points out the correlation between anger and danger: they are closely related in how they work together to defend you. Anytime a threat, problem, injustice, opposition, or malicious event occurs, your mind and body trigger a sophisticated alarm system to help produce an emergency response. Like a fire alarm, your mind and body alert you to follow the signal to safety. Anger is your friend.

We become alerted when we see a construction worker carelessly swing heavy equipment near a small child. We automatically initiate a "fight or flight" response focused on helping the potential victim. We spring into action. Whether the threat of pain is directed at us or someone else, our response towards danger – real or perceived – may surface as anger. Bretherick refers to anger as a God-given response to produce what he calls "anger energy" in our bodies. In the same context in chapter 4, we discussed a neurologically activated physical response within our bodies. Bretherick proposes we need to recognize that anger triggers the energy within our bodies that drives us to respond appropriately to injustices.

When we change the way we think about anger, it helps us to ask what is causing the "smoke detector" to go off rather than ignoring the anger stimuli. The frown, clenched teeth, tight fists, and breaking a sweat are all important physical responses that might seem threatening. We need to learn to listen to our bodies and channel anger energy into a better response rather than stewing, pouting, or seething in anger.

Dave and Jeanine are a successful couple and are influential leaders in their community. Dave had a relatively normal childhood; you would not know on the surface that there had ever been any problems. He has had a very successful life and has been a caring dad nurturing well-balanced kids. He has a great career as an architectural designer and has received professional awards and acknowledgements for his work. Having a good sense of humor, Dave can easily carry the conversation with entertaining stories and clever anecdotes in any context, professional or social.

Before counselling, Dave would not have admitted that his mother was controlling and manipulative. She was often mean-spirited, but only behind closed doors. Consequently, Dave became increasingly angry as he grew up. Even though he mellowed through the years, his kids remember how he used to snap. His tongue could readily be the life of the party and just as easily lash out at his staff, wife, or kids. Unfortunately, Dave could be brutally vicious both in the tone and content of his comments. His kids had difficulty emerging into their teen years because as a dad, he had left his kids timid victims of his anger. Dave repeated the anger he experienced. It took him decades to begin to forgive his mother – a process he is still working through.

Many individuals struggle with similar anger issues resulting from childhood experiences within their family. It is preferred to deny or suppress injustices or violations of our wellbeing that trigger our anger responses. Behaviors – both good and bad – are often modeled from generation to generation. For example, behaviors expressed by our grandparents are often seen in our parents. Eventually, these good and bad behaviors can be mimicked by the children of these parents. Sooner or later, someone needs to stop the cycle of bad behavior and acknowledge the behavior that needs to change, such as anger, and actually deal with it.

Although Dave's anger has not erupted for years, his family remembers what it used to be like. They are still affected by it. As a result, he is not very close to his kids; they are still emotionally unavailable to each other.

When anger comes to the surface, it reveals that something deep is happening below the surface, just like a volcano. If Dave's anger were to remain as a threatening volcano with everyone cautiously awaiting an eruption, then there is no chance to develop healthy communication. If Dave puts in the effort, recovery is possible.

Anger is our friend when we utilize this alarm and ask, "What danger is this anger revealing? What caused it? Is this the problem or is there some deeper historical issue lingering beneath it?" The right questions lead us away from our anger and help us to move towards forgiveness. Forgiveness is not just a one-time act; it also is a process. Significant changes occur when anger and resentment subside when we make forgiveness an ongoing lifestyle choice.

We can process anger much more safely with the use of questions. Frank's wife had been angry on numerous occasions since they got married. As a husband and her best friend, Frank tried to be wise and cautious when approaching her when he saw or heard signs that the anger "smoke alarm" had gone off. He attentively and respectfully asked her, "Can you help me understand what you are so angry about?" In spite of all his wisdom and years of experience living with her in marriage, Frank still had a hard time hearing the response: "I'm mad because of you! I'm upset with what you said... what you did!"

When she chose to be upset, Frank needed to make a choice to not focus on what she said. She made a choice to be upset. If he took responsibility for her feelings, he would feel bad and beaten down even before they start a discussion. However, if Frank saw beyond the emotion, he would be able to create an opportunity to reveal the source of her anger. Frank did not have to take it personally because it was not about him. He did not have to be defensive, but could keep asking questions. Maybe there was some validity to what she said. Frank could help her get to the bottom of what was causing her to feel upset.

It sounds obvious, but if the literal smoke detector goes off because someone burned the toast, the solution is not to call the fire department. The remedy is not to evacuate the house. Resolution is not found in discharging the contents of the fire extinguisher all around the kitchen. When the alarm goes off, all we need to really do is look around to see what the problem is. We can sort out the issue with a moment of attention, and move on. Anger *can* be like that. We just need to think about anger differently.

Anger and its accompanying anxiety are emotional signals that help create the understanding of how we filter and/or work through those filters in the communication process. We do not have to feel injured and sulk for hours or days at a time. We can simply acknowledge the feelings and choose to move on and *not* take it personally.

When we do not work through these emotions, they impede the communication process. Symbolically, a dirty, unchanged furnace filter can lead to furnace damage, or an unchanged car thermostat can cause the engine to overheat and malfunction. Both of these pending issues are often brought to our attention by a warning indicator light, yet the fix is simple. The furnace filter and car thermostat are inexpensive parts that keep things moving and functioning well. Ultimately, that is all an emotional spike in our anger needs to be: a quick "indicator light" that flashes on and off to get our attention to deal with the problem. We can choose to ignore it, or we can choose to remain calm and resolve it.

Unresolved anger can lead to other problems as well such as headaches, ulcers, Crohn's disease, ulcerative colitis, high blood pressure, cancer, anorexia, bulimia, overeating, and structural problems.[7] Beyond the inherent health issues, unresolved anger could lead to hardness of the heart or bitterness.

Temporary insanity

In their book *How God Changes Your Brain*, Andrew Newberg and Mark Robert Waldman describe some of the difficulty we have controlling our anger and how it contributes to communication breakdown. Of course, when anger escalates during communication, it only exacerbates the situation. The authors state that "anger interrupts the functioning of your frontal lobes. Not only do you lose the ability to be rational, you lose the awareness that you're acting in an irrational way."[8] Further, they say that as anger increases and your frontal lobes stop functioning, it is no longer possible to even hear what the other person is saying or even feel the compassion, sympathy, or empathy we should. "Instead," they write, "you are likely to feel self-justified and self-righteous and when that happens the communication process falls apart," and as if things weren't bad enough, the heightened rage releases a host of neurochemicals that "actually destroy those parts of the brain that control emotional reactivity."[9] Consequently, we literally and neurologically shut down our emotions.

Until we retrain our minds to think about more positive things, it is as though we lose control of our minds in moments of anger. Science supports that this "temporary insanity" of anger is a very real occurrence. Instead, we must focus on our moral, ethical, and even religious values to act kindly – to think kind thoughts, in order to reverse the effects of unhealthy thoughts and heal our minds.

Impenetrable barrier

I know I am not immune to this temporary insanity or beyond getting angry in some form, nor am I trying to deny the existence of or avoid anger. Instead, I am learning to utilize anger as a signal to indicate areas in my relationships or life that need to be identified and worked on. Consider working *with* your anger instead of denying it or resisting it. What about others in your life? Do not avoid them when they are angry. Work *with* them, if you can, to resolve the anger.

Being upset or ticked does not have to be the end of the relationship. Further, not everything that stirs anger is a deal-breaker. Just because I am angry does not mean I cannot explore *why* I am angry. Anger does not have to become an impenetrable barrier to communication.

Therapeutic resistance

Here is the deeper issue. Every time a person is confronted about their anger or hostility, it can serve to be just another brick in the wall.

The term "therapeutic resistance" initially comes from the medical world. Globally, antibiotics have been misused and overused and, consequently, have become less effective. Many diseases traditionally treated by penicillin have built up resistance to this antibiotic. The same phenomenon affects cancer treatment. The disease builds a wall against the therapy.

Similarly, we also see a measure of resistance in the diagnosis and treatment of anger.

Dave, our aforementioned friend, had it pointed out to him for many years that he was angry. He heard it from his wife. His colleagues mentioned his temper problem to him as well. His performance reviews also addressed Dave's issue with anger. His wife Jeanine would often refer to Dave "being on his best behavior" when family visits or special occasions necessitated that Dave's mood not become the center of attention.

Continually exasperated by people telling him he was grouchy or irritable, Dave got angrier. He learned to control the anger on the surface, but never really resolved any of the underlying issues. He started his own company to avoid the former workplace tension. He moved his home to a totally different neighborhood and changed churches to escape previous conflicts. Although he changed his life for a fresh start, he was neither happier nor content. When he faced some personal health issues, he started to take inventory of all the people who upset him. He began to forgive, to let people off the hook, and to cancel the metaphoric "debts" of those who had wronged him. Dave was beginning to actually change himself from the inside.

This reflects the common cycle of anger. Many people resist confrontation when they are continually being challenged by someone else regarding their anger, but their resistance causes greater problems than necessary. Many who struggle with anger continue to grow angrier. They deny it, rationalize it, or hide behind some other defense mechanism, but the spiral of anger continues to grow unchecked. When it is not consistently addressed, it only seems to make the person angrier, grouchier, meaner, more irritable, or more defensive.

Countless clients parallel Dave, who feel they are at the end of their rope with respect to their anger. Some act out by engaging in behaviors such as addiction, infidelity, or cruel gossip. Others become passive-aggressive, often expressed by a lifestyle of procrastination, sarcasm, teasing, pouting, non-compliance, road rage, or job loss.

Because anger can express these character flaws, some clients have just grown tired of feeling lousy about themselves. Others cannot find the root causes of their frustrations, depression, or self-loathing. They need not wait for a health crisis or any other tragedy before dealing with anger.

Thankfully, there is a better way to get to the heart of this potentially destructive emotion. No one needs to become a drug addict or an alcoholic or divorced before finally changing. In every case, the way begins with questions:

- "What are you angry about today?"
- "Can you talk about those feelings?"
- "What things or people have made you angry recently?"
- "Have you forgiven them?"
- "Can you *choose* to forgive them?"
- "Who are you hurting when you choose *not* to forgive them?"
- "What steps would it take to forgive them?"
- "Are there things you need to say to someone?"
- "Could you perhaps write a letter expressing your feelings?"
- "Can you think of a time earlier in life where you felt these same feelings?"
- "Is there something or someone from years ago that you still might need to forgive?"
- "Can you briefly describe what happened in each case?"
- "What will it take to forgive them?"
- "Can you finally just simply forgive? Can you release each person of their "debt" to you?"
- "Is there possibility of, or a need for, reconciliation?"
- "Can you forgive yourself?"

Working through this list of questions is a process, which might only take a few hours or days for some emotionally aware individuals. However, for others who may have layers upon layers of hurt, pain, and woundedness, it might take months or even years to uncover the source of hurt and pain.

Stonewalling and gridlock

Dr. John M. Gottman is a psychologist and professor known for presenting and propagating the term "stonewaller." In his book *The Seven Principles for Making Marriages Work*, he also uses the term "gridlock" to describe a similar concept.[10] To stonewall is what you might expect: to refuse to respond, to go quiet, to clam up emotionally, not expressing thoughts or feelings. Men tend to stonewall more than women. Stonewalling is often tied to unexpressed, unresolved anger. Many couples will see a measure of stonewalling because issues are not being resolved. "Gridlock" describes the state of communication in which they find themselves when they are unable to resolve a recurring conflict. Gottman calls the recurring conflict a perpetual problem and he proposes that 69% of relationship conflict stems from unresolvable issues. Whether because of differences of opinion or differences in personalities, couples will spin their wheels and go nowhere. The result is gridlock.

Gottman goes on to say that the only way to resolve gridlock is to focus on a different kind of resolution:

to manage conflict instead.[11] For example, if a wife and husband feel they have been heard deeply and completely by each other, they do not even need resolution on any perpetual issue. What they really crave and desire is a perceived level of understanding and acceptance. They need their spouse to say things like, "I care" or "I appreciate…." They do not need to hear from each other, "I'm trying to change your values to mine; I want you to adapt to my point of view." Gottman suggests that if partners can accept and remove the emotional barriers that come between them, they can get along and function well in marriage in spite of significant differences of opinion.

Marv was known in college as "Poker Face." When asked about anything philosophical, risky, or especially issues of the heart, emotions, or feelings, Marv would just clam up and not say a word. He might change the subject or joke it off, but most often, he would just stonewall.

Marv came by it honestly. His stepfather was an Irish immigrant who would joke about "Pint Therapy." If his dad had a rough day at work, he prided himself on not complaining to his family or taking it out on them. He would stop by the pub on the way home, have a pint and keep his mouth shut, not drinking away his sorrows, but just remaining silent over a pint or two while he locked up his true feelings. Being raised in that environment was what predominantly influenced Marv to become a stonewaller. The stonewalling did not come as a surprise to Sheila, his wife, who knew his nickname while they dated, but he seemed to be a happy-go-lucky guy most of the time. Stonewalling never was an issue the first several years of marriage. After having three kids, the dynamics and tensions of the marriage changed, gradually but significantly. When Marv was really upset, he would fume and even pout for days at a time. When Sheila asked what the problem was, he would clam up and stare off into space.

Sheila, by contrast, worked in gridlock, which occurs when a person may talk about an issue, perhaps even the feelings around an issue, but not resolve anything regarding the issue. Things were either avoided (stonewall) by Marv or revisited on many occasions by Sheila (gridlock) but never healed or resolved.

Both gridlock and stonewalling are relationship killers. Even the best imaginable questions can be terribly timed. If Sheila were to ask, "Marv, you're stonewalling right now, aren't you? Is this your poker face? Are you clamming up again?" it would only serve to escalate the problem. Sometimes, if not asked properly or with improper motivation, a question may be an accusation in disguise. Or even worse, a question can be an accusation *without* a disguise. In subsequent chapters, we will talk about leading people to the truth by asking questions, not ambushing them! As well, we will touch on timing and time-out issues to make questions more effective. Do not jump into questions without the whole story because it could easily do more harm than good.

When Marv and Sheila did finally seek counselling, a sense of "it is safe to share" was established. Conversations felt safe to Marv. Simple questions like, "Marv, I've noticed that you don't respond to any of the questions I've asked of you. Can you talk about what has happened in your life that is causing you to withhold your response?" and, "How was anger and conflict dealt with in your family of origin?" were answered by Marv because he felt safe. Marv recounted his stepdad stonewalling because, from Marv's point of view, his stepdad did not know how to respond to his wife when she got angry. Marv felt that his stepfather was not respected or loved by Marv's mother when he talked. As a young boy, Marv came to conclude that the same would hold true for him. Marv believed that it was better to not say anything than to open your mouth and be criticized for what you say. In addition, Marv had experienced trauma in his late childhood that was never properly resolved or managed. He had not been heard. His stepfather had never been heard either. He had made a promise to himself as a young teenager that he would never open his mouth because of the trouble that follows.

Sheila was asked if she respected and loved Marv enough to allow him to be open with his feelings. When Sheila shared her affirmative answer, she reached out and embraced Marv so warmly that he started to cry as though he had held back his feelings for decades. Truth be told, he *had* held back his feelings for decades, especially his negative emotions.

As this couple progressed, Marv talked about the continual gridlock of stalled emotions Sheila had shared, feelings that she could not navigate on her own. Sheila also poorly managed the negativity she felt toward Marv. It often seemed like Sheila was accusing him of failure or wrongdoing. Because Sheila could not move ahead without discussion, she perpetually revisited the feelings that made Marv feel worthless. It was a catch-22. He only resolved to clam up more.

As the process continued, Marv learned to trust Sheila with his feelings more openly. She learned to listen and to reflect back his words and feelings. Reflecting back, Marv's words helped him to know that Sheila was hearing him. Sheila happily said later, "It took years, but now he shares everything with me! He even pulls ideas, thoughts, and emotions out of me and helps me process things."

Anger awareness

Once we have worked through the defense mechanisms listed in chapter 7, we can move past the emotional barriers that limit relationships. We can see beyond the masks and get a glimpse of who we really are. I believe questions are the best tool to help ourselves, our friends, and our families to realize the truth about our anger issues. Questions can stimulate us to think about our thoughts and the reasons that impeded resolving the emotional resistance.

I recently met with Brent, a sharp, affable young man. He would never say anything bad about anyone or anything. He had come to see me because he had confessed something to his girlfriend that they both concluded was inappropriate. They both felt he should talk to a counsellor about it. Brent told me that he goes on the internet to look at women in bondage.

I asked Brent if he ever felt angry. Brent could not remember anything in particular. He could not think of anything he was angry, upset, or bothered about. As I kept asking questions, Brent and I both realized that he had reasons to be angry, but he never did become overtly angry. We came to realize that his inability to express his anger in an overt way was very problematic. There had been a high level of latent, unresolved anger in his life. He admitted that seeing women in bondage was an outlet for expressing his anger.

Generally, pornography is an expression of anger. It is not just harmless "art" or "entertainment." This subjugation of women is a global pandemic because many men of this generation have not learned to express anger in a healthy manner.

For Brent, he felt excitement and relief from whatever the anger that left him feeling not so good. By feeling that he had a measure of control – in this case, over women – the negative feelings were suppressed. His sexual arousal felt good, sufficiently blocking out any guilt or other negative feelings.

Because Brent had difficulty identifying the source of his anger, he enlisted the help of his parents without divulging the reason, asking them what might be the cause of his anger. For others, an anger log, an anger inventory, or lots of questions about anger can help them tune in to the source of their anger. Then, and only then, do they have potential to change.

Nothing to fear, not even fear itself

In the story of Marv, we saw anecdotally that fear can manifest as anger. Marv was afraid of not being accepted. He had an established fear of rejection dating back to the days of seeing his father get yelled at by his mother when his father dared to make a comment. Marv's fear was reinforced through trauma when he tried communicating but was not heard. He developed a fear of not being heard again, and he was angry about it.

Many times, angry people are simply trying to get a reaction. Sometimes anger can signal various underlying fears such as fear of failure, rejection, pain, disappointment, being hurt, and many other possibilities. The angry person might only want to make something else happen. For them, desperate times call for desperate measures. Some think that if they yell louder, things will change. So for the angry person, self-awareness of anger helps dramatically. The more aware you are of your own anger or someone else's, the more intelligent questions you can ask.

Shame

Rosa had been sober for almost 20 years. The first 15 years of her marriage with Art had been a nightmare, but they mostly survived that rocky start. Rosa and Art had managed to have two fine, healthy kids in spite of her addiction. A few close calls with the kids' safety finally caused Rosa to participate in a 12-step recovery program called "Scared Straight." Specifically, a minor fender-bender while slightly under the influence was the lowest point that awakened her to getting help; both kids were with her in the car at the time. Rosa stopped drinking the same night as that traumatic incident, but unfortunately, she only put a band-aid on the problem. Her deeper issue was that she received little respect from her father. Consequently, Rosa was not a big fan of men, not even of Art.

As a result, Rosa had a nasty streak. She attacked and belittled Art with her razor-sharp tongue, sometimes in public; I can only imagine what things were like at home. Art said that once, and only once, he "had enough" (his own words). While on a business trip one time, Art got inappropriately involved with a recently divorced woman from a partner company – not sexually, but emotionally. Art was immediately remorseful, and he apologized to Rosa, but 10 years later, there were still unresolved emotions around the issue.

Rosa despised the woman with whom her husband had engaged in an emotional tryst. She had never met or seen her, but loathed her nonetheless. As Rosa sat in my office, I could tell she was uncomfortable dialoguing about *her* issues that had hurt their marriage. Although there was mutual agreement that we would briefly explore her past, she wanted the focus off of her as soon as possible.

She was hurting, she wanted Art to hurt too, and she knew exactly what buttons to push. "Yeah," she lashed out defensively. "I've made some mistakes... but at least I didn't get involved with someone." You could visibly see the wind fade from Art's sails. He felt deflated and turned white in the span of five seconds. He was trying desperately to do his part to hold his marriage together.

"You're right!" he immediately replied. "I'm the problem here."

In this conflict, Rosa had belittled her partner with shame.

Shame off you

Shame is an overwhelming feeling that can control people, modify the course of their lives and even ruin them. Like fear and anger, shame has a healthy and unhealthy side.

Healthy shame shows me that "I was late for work. It was a mistake." The mistake motivates me to leave for work earlier tomorrow to compensate. Unhealthy shame says, "I'm late again. I can't get anything right. I *am* a mistake."

Sometimes, especially in the middle of a conflict when we're being belittled, shame only makes us feel more fearful, abandoned, helpless, or hopeless. When I am already feeling ashamed, the conflict only adds to a fear of being alone. Shame and fear are often travelling companions – often finding one on the coattails of the other.

The good news is that shame, like fear, can rationally and methodically be deconstructed with the right questions. The superlatives and over-generalizations of shame, such as, "you always mess up, you're never good enough, you don't measure up, you deserve this, you'll never amount to anything," can be changed with a positive twist that makes one think about their thinking!

- "Do I mess up every time, or does it just feel like that?"

- "Am I good enough? Why not?"
- "Have I succeeded at some things? "What things specifically?"
- "Have there been specific times where I *have* been good enough?"
- "Haven't I helped others?"
- "Have I been sucked into feeling sorry for myself?"
- "Am I believing a lie?"
- "What positive sayings, ideas, or thoughts can I remind myself of to get out of this negativity? "
- "How does God feel about me? What does He think of me?"

Ron was an educated man with a lovely wife, a son, a daughter, and a successful engineering career. After getting laid off in his mid-50s and receiving a good severance package, he felt he still needed to work another four or five years before he could afford to retire at his current level of comfort. However, it took him three years to find another job. The extended time off between jobs took a toll on him. He could have retired at 60 if his previous employer had retained him, but now retirement was looking to be deferred to age 65.

Ron struggled with low self-esteem, feelings of shame, and worthlessness. He was diagnosed as being mild to moderately depressed and he was medicated accordingly. Ron still struggled with depression even after finding a more desirable job with better money and more flexibility fit. The meds seemed to help a bit, but it took a blend of cognitive behavior therapy coupled with the medication to get him through this season of life.

During counselling, Ron tracked his discouragement to a recurring source of shame. Ron had feelings of inferiority and shame growing up in his family, but he overcame much of that discouragement by finding his niche in university studies. This average high school student had gone unnoticed by his secondary school teachers, but blossomed studying engineering in university. He had found an avenue of success. He tied his identity to his engineering career. It was successful and fulfilling for him. Even though he had struggled with periods of depression throughout his adult life, they always seemed to be short-term and manageable. In his words, he would "get back to normal" every time. However, this time was different. The issue was that shame had deeply taken root in his mind.

For Ron, the operative word for shame was "normal." He felt he had been average and normal all of his growing up years. Only when he excelled in school and later in his career did he feel above average. Only when he could retire at 60 instead of 65 did he feel above average. For him, average was shameful. But then came the questions:

- So what?
- So what if you retire at 65 instead of 60?

- What if you retire with an average pension and RRSPs instead of above average?
- Is it the end of the world?
- Could you downsize and still have a wonderful life?
- Does your wife still love you?
- Do you have fabulous and amazingly successful kids?
- So what that you got laid off?
- Isn't your new job what you had always dreamed of?
- Isn't it better to go into retirement on a high note instead of hating your work?
- Isn't this a step-up more than a set-back?
- Can you have fun at work again? (Something he hadn't had in a decade.)

After many sessions where questions were asked and answers processed, Ron began to feel fulfilled and at peace with himself and his job. Ron had nothing to prove – either to himself or others.

Chapter 9

The many faces of inquiry

"If there are no stupid questions, then what
kind of questions do stupid people ask? Do
they get smart just in time to ask questions?"
– Scott Adams

As I have been discussing throughout this book, questions are an incredibly useful tool in communication. A vast array of questions can be utilized to increase understanding and to give you an advantage in communication when you learn to use them. You just need to be aware of what types of questions are at your disposal.

Types of questions

There are five primary kinds of questions: convergent, rhetorical, dichotomous, qualifying, and divergent. Often, they create a sixth hybrid option: the "combination" questions that utilize two or more components of the five types listed.

Convergent questions

Convergent questions evoke answers that converge on one simple truth, a "right" answer, even when it is your personal opinion. They are also known as "factual" questions or "knowledge acquisition" questions, such as, "What is your name?" This is not very complicated. Unless you frequently use a pseudonym or a middle name, you do not really need to qualify this question. Most people get the answer right away. Thus, the goal of convergent questions is to elicit that one possible answer.

The emergency room doctor asks this common question of individuals presenting with a head injury: "How many fingers am I holding up?" He is not trying to trick them. There is no deep philosophical point to this, seeking to differentiate between the real and the surreal or perceived. He just wants to know if your vision has been affected by your injury. When asked, "What color is the sky?" most people will conform to generally convergent thought by responding, "Blue." Likewise, there is no need to add, "if it's not cloudy at midday."

Another example of the use of convergent questions is found in the journalism practice of inquiry through the traditional five W and H questions: Who? What? Where?

When? Why? How? Generally speaking, asking these six unique convergent questions results in a comprehensive survey of every situation. The more people you ask, the greater the convergent perspective you obtain. Even though eyewitnesses – either by the roadside, on the hill, or on top of the building – may offer vastly different answers to those six questions, a good reporter can reach a fairly accurate conclusion.

Dichotomous questions

The ancient Greek word "Dicho" means "two parts." "Tome" means "to cut" or "divide." A dichotomous question most often stems from the convergent family where one answer is possible, yet the respondent is given two options, such as "yes" or "no," "true" or "false." The point is not for the responder to say, "It's both true and false!" A teacher, for example, will instruct the student to circle the one that is most correct and move on.

Rhetorical questions

A rhetorical question comes from the root word "rhetoric," having to do with language. Rhetorical questions are more intended to evoke an effect, to make a point or a comment, not expecting an answer. "There's nothing as exhilarating as a walk by the river is there?"

The answer assumed or intended is for agreement: "Yes, you're right. It's very pleasant to walk by the river." The conversation is mere rhetoric, or rhetorical. The question politely assumes agreement and support of the comment. The one asking presumes you will not argue or debate. The point is not for you to respond "That's foolishness! A walk by the lake or in the woods is far superior!" Nevertheless, a rhetorical question is a polite way of making a statement, even a bold or possibly contentious statement that invites others into consensus.

Qualifying questions

Qualifying questions filter out possible answers and broaden the range of choice. Such questions are also called "filter questions," "choice" or "multiple choice questions," or "range questions." For example, "Do you watch TV?" is a simple convergent, factual, dichotomous closed-ended question. It requires a simple yes or no. However, the next question, "How much TV do you watch each day?" could have a variety or range of choices: One hour a day? Two? Three? More than three?

Qualifying questions such as, "How much TV do you watch each day?" add factual support to the first question. One who watches TV can easily identify a realistic amount of daily TV viewing to help the inquirer better understand their TV viewing habits.

Multiple choice questions found in surveys and tests are also examples of qualifying questions, or "range" questions. Other range questions include scale questions, such as "On a scale of 1 to 10 where 1 is terrible and 10 is excellent, how did you like the food at this restaurant?" In any case, your options for choosing are limited.

Perhaps you have noticed the language of "closed-ended" and "open-ended" questions referred to above. If we oversimplify questions into those two types, the preceding questions would all be examples of close-ended questions which lead the respondent into a narrow possibility of answers, with limited considerations, the answers brief and pointed. Like a conversation between a teenager and their parent, the parent asks a lot of questions, which have short answer possibilities:

Parent: Teenager:
"Where were you?"   "Out."
"What time did you get in?"   "Late."
"Who were you with?"   "Friends."
"Which ones?"   "The usual."

This dialogue is a recipe for frustration. The parent wants to know more and is bothered by the lack of communication, yet is asking only close-ended questions.

Divergent questions

Divergent questions are open-ended questions. In the list of five W questions, an open-ended or divergent question will focus continually on the "why?" Divergent questions are also called "conceptual questions." They are more concerned with the broader concept than with the details. They focus on the macro more than the micro. Where convergent questions have only limited answers, divergent questions offer an endless variety of responses.

Interestingly, education and developmental studies tell us that under the age of five, approximately 95% of children naturally function in divergent thinking, while only 5% tend towards convergent thinking. As children progress through the education system, they change. In his book *The Artisan* Soul, author Erwin McManus suggests the following:

> "The worldview that we transfer to our children is that there is always only one right answer to every problem, and that answer has already been discovered by your teacher...You must excel at memorizing the facts that your teacher already knows, so that one day you may teach them to someone else."[12]

Great teachers embrace a divergent approach to education. They open up vast possibilities in learning, teaching their students how to learn. Others embrace a more antiquated system of learning, by rote and repetition, where students merely accumulate knowledge. I believe there is a place for rote and repetition, but there needs to be opportunity for learning how to *learn*.

Noted 18th century American author and educator Alice Wellington Rollins says, "The test of a good teacher is not how many questions he can ask his pupils that they will answer readily, but how many questions he inspires them to ask him which he finds it hard to answer."[13] Much is reflected in the fact that the term "divergent" has strong negative implications. Creativity and individuality are seen as enemies of the convergent school of thought. Divergent thinking stimulates open-mindedness and overcomes the closed-minded defensiveness that undermines healthy relationships.

These are several reasons we celebrate open-ended questions. They pull us out of a linear, sequential, Western mindset and facilitate a more global, broad-spectrum, divergent way of thinking. The closed-ended question asks, "Do you have any family?" It shows interest in someone you just met. It shows that you want to know more about them. A better option is a question that opens the door to conversational possibility without limits. The first question could be answered, "Yes, I have family." The door is partially open to fill in the blank, but a better, more open-ended question would be, "I would love to know more about your family. What are they like?"

Closed-ended questions look for specific details. "What's your name? Where are you from? What do you do for a living? Are you married? Do you have kids? How old are they? What part of the city do you live in? Where do your kids go to school? Where did you go to school? What was your major in university? How long have you worked for this company? Where is your spouse from? Where did you meet?" Although these are good questions to ask, closed-ended questions only elicit a response telling what I want to know, not necessarily what they want to tell me.

By way of contrast, you can replace all of the above questions with, "How would you describe yourself to me, meeting you for the first time? What is your story?" With that question, people who answer have inexhaustible options with which to respond, but more importantly, they can choose to prioritize what *they* think is important in their reply. A great follow-up question that invites people to think about themselves is, "What would your friends say about you if I asked them?" It also gives them the freedom to say wonderful things about themselves without being accused of bragging. Open-ended questioning removes limits from dead-end "yes" or "no" questions in a conversation.

Why does this matter in a marriage? Because marriage is like going to the gym. If you want to keep your marriage healthy, intentional work is required to help it grow. When you ask your spouse open-ended questions, you get to know them better. To facilitate the area of relationship development, I often refer to the books *1,000 Questions for Couples* by Michael Webb or *Just Ask! 1,000 Questions to Grow Your Relationship* by Michele O'Mara.

Chapter 10

Tools used with questions to impact relationship growth

"The single biggest problem in communication
is the illusion that it has taken place."
– George Bernard Shaw

Obviously, questions are not the answer to every conversational and relational problem. Both communication and relationships can break down. When either falls apart abruptly, it can seem irreparable. There is an underpinning of foundational relational strength and stability that questions can help establish at a deeper level. Hopefully, where relational strength is deeply entrenched, even amid conflict, misunderstanding, unmet expectations, or disappointment, the relationship will survive, if it is strongly built on mutual respect and care.

The following are other components of relationship that provide a better understanding of emotional health.

Acceptance and belonging

We all want acceptance. We all want to belong. The need for acceptance and belonging motivates us to seek out relationships. We join community organizations, churches, and sports teams to satisfy this desire. For those who do not have the sense of acceptance and belonging, they feel lonely, out of place, and even rejected. To ask someone their thoughts, opinions, or feelings brings affirmation and inclusion. Caring inquiries communicate feelings of both acceptance and belonging.

To ask or not to ask?

Usually, you listen and ask questions because you care. Asking questions breaks down barriers. To not ask may send a message that you do not care and tends to build relational walls and barriers. However, some people just do not know how to direct a conversation. A deeper level of conversation is accessed through probing questions – but this probing must be done with care. When questions are accompanied with a suspect feeling of being nosy or seeking dirt on another person, most people can discern the negativity and won't respond to such questions.

Tanya came to my office looking for help. She was fundamentally distrusting. When I asked initial questions of inventory to learn her story, she shot back, "Why do you ask?" I explained that, to help her the best I could, I needed to know her story. Like many other clients, she softened and settled into the conversational flow created by my series of routine questions. The conversation became easier as Tanya learned to trust the process.

Contrast: Real world versus my office

Imagine how awkward the atmosphere would be if, when welcoming new clients into my office, I invited them to sit in a comfortable chair, then just stared at my notepad and said nothing. Or, if we small talked for a couple minutes and I took notes for five minutes. This is the opposite of the environment I am trying to create.

Wanting to establish a place of safety, I chat briefly with clients about some easy subject like the weather, a current event, a family story, anything to bring them a sense of familiarity and comfort. I then channel the conversation in a professional direction. I walk first-time clients through a series of inventory questions such as "Who referred you?" "Have you attended counselling previously?" "Do you understand the confidentiality form you are signing?" Whether a first-time visit or the tenth visit, the discussion begins with a question such as, "What do you want to talk about today?" From there, clients feel more comfortable to share, which gives me insight into their lives. They expect that I will ask questions.

Successful communication must be shared. In my office, I do not ask a client, "Why don't you ask about me?" The focus falls upon the patient. Outside the counselling office, communication is expected to be a shared experience, not one-sided. Those with poor conversational skills who only talk about themselves and do not ask questions to get to know others, or those who are shy, selfish, or narcissistic, often have difficulty reciprocating, and may respond disrespectfully when relating to others. When questions are asked, it balances a conversation and creates interaction.

Accountability

In the ancient biblical story of creation, God confronts the actions of the first man and woman, Adam and Eve. They managed to break the one rule He gave them: do not eat the fruit of the tree of the knowledge of good and evil. They did eat it.

According to the Genesis account, God and Adam talked regularly. One day, when God was in the garden, He looked for Adam, calling out for him. But Adam was hiding because he felt ashamed. The all-knowing, everywhere present God asked Adam, "Where are you?"

Adam responded, "I am hiding because I was naked and afraid."

God then asks, "Who told you that you were naked? Did you eat any fruit from that tree in the middle of the garden? What have you done?" The outcome? Adam and Eve became self-aware and experienced the impact of their thoughts and actions: getting evicted from the Garden of Eden.

God calls them into account and asks for answers, even though He already knew the answers to His own questions. God's questions are not about gathering information. Rather, He is helping Adam and Eve to become self-aware and accountable. By asking them to give an account for their actions, God directs them to know and face the facts.

Is anyone above accountability?

A consultant was hired to evaluate a charitable organization in Europe. His role was to review the inner workings of the organization with the intent of making recommendations for moving forward. To begin, he asked many questions about how things worked within the organization including roles and job descriptions. Further, to get an understanding of the systems and structures that were in place, he explored who was accountable to whom. During the process, as they sorted through the organizational flow chart, the consultant shared a story of a very large and famous charitable organization in America that had hired him to help set up structures and improve their overall organizational impact. This organization had already experienced significant decline years earlier when the CEO had engaged in unscrupulous behaviors. It lost 80% of its support and influence. Accordingly, the American charity's effectiveness dwindled.

As the consultant inquired about accountability structures within the American charitable organization, he asked the Executive Director about the CEO, a famous, internationally recognized personality. The first question he asked was, "Who says 'no' to the boss?"

The Executive Director mirrored back incredulously, "What? Who says 'no' to the boss?" then chuckled. The Executive Director said that he wanted the gentleman to ask that question directly to the CEO. He took the consultant in to meet the boss where the consultant was sarcastically asked to pose the same question to the CEO directly.

The consultant proceeded to ask the CEO, "Who says 'no' to you?"

The CEO and Executive Director laughed. With a puzzled look, the consultant asked what was so funny. The response of the Executive Director was simply, "Nobody says 'no' to the boss!" With that understanding, the consultant left. He walked away from the job because he was fully aware that he could not help an organization where there was no genuine accountability. The boss remained accountable to no one and the charity eventually became a shadow of its former stature.

Questions hold people accountable. Raising questions of accountability engages the process of discerning and creates accountable structures, systems, and relationships. Traditionally, human beings rebel against accountability, in part because it appears as manipulative control, and people resent control. However, the greatest benefits of accountability arise when the best intentions flow from the heart.

Accountability tests trust. Accountability comes across as invasive or demanding because it lacks compassion. Trust will not grow without compassion. If the purposes of accountability are to be achieved, compassion must be included. When others are honest, transparent, and genuine, we can trust them to improve many areas of relationships. More loving, deeper questions should increase personal and relational accountability. Through accountability, we develop a healthier sense of self. In turn, healthier relationships result from responding well instead of reacting to others. Compassion helps bring things to light, and accountability helps to build it right. Compassionate inquiry will improve relationships through time.

Remember Clay and Fran from Chapter 6? Clay struggled with self-pity and attempted to rewire his brain away from it. He started to understand that Fran was *not* trying to destroy him. When his victim mentality perceived that anything he did was wrong, he needlessly defended himself against her "attacks." When Fran asked, "Am I attacking you? Are you perceiving this as an attack? Are you feeling like a victim?" she was calling him to be accountable for his feelings, thoughts, and actions. Her reminders helped him deconstruct his victim mentality by facilitating a new understanding that the world is not out to get him. The misperceptions caused by his birth family no longer hurt him. Instead, they are considered to be inaccurate. His internal mental messages are changing substantially. Therefore, how Clay relates to Fran is also changing. What he thinks and feels has changed because of accountability. Clay was being challenged to be mindful about unhealthy negative perspectives.

As we continued to diminish Clay's fear of rejection and challenged him to be more accountable for his false beliefs about Fran rejecting him, Clay became more positive. He felt less alone, less isolated. Through counselling, new evidence emerged for Clay to process. Tough questions were asked, but they were spoken with kindness. Accountability-type questions led Clay towards the truth and pulled him away from emotionally based responses and into metacognitive processing. At the end of the day, he was better able to see the facts.

The admirable thing about the process is that Clay is now self-managing himself as he overcomes his rejection issues. Further, when he feels manipulated or hurt, he asks himself the accountability question, "Has she actually said I'm not good enough?" His true beliefs are exposed. There is a direct correlation: as Clay internally manages his accountability, his relationship with Fran, as well as with other people, improves.

True accountability is designed to improve behavior and relationships. The person who *does not want* to be accountable wants to protect their fear, perhaps even their isolation. They want to be in control. As people acknowledge and take responsibility for their negative and destructive behaviors and endeavor to correct them, bad behavior turns to good behavior. Wrongs are made right.

Accountability plays a substantial role in the process of gaining understanding, especially in how we perceive one another. Relationships face many roadblocks. Primarily, fear blocks deeper relationships, specifically, the fear of being rejected. The flip side is the need within us for acceptance, as mentioned at the beginning of this chapter. Some people become critical of others due to fear of rejection. Believing that they are not good enough, they reject others before they get rejected. Conversely, others function as "people pleasers" in order to be accepted.

Todd and Benni are a couple with a unique story. Todd's mother was bipolar, so he grew up in a very unstable single-parent home. His mother's behavior depended upon whether she took her medication and if it was effective. As an 11-year-old, Todd had to grow up quickly, taking on the responsibility of helping to run the household, making up for his mother's emotional absence. As an adult, he walked a thin line between focusing on himself, to make up for his lost teen years when he wanted to hang out with his friends, and endeavoring to be a man of great responsibility, as was expected of him even at age 11.

Benni's mom carried suppressed resentment and seething anger. Her dad was a nice man, but a pushover. Benni would do almost anything to make her parents happy. A "golden child," Benni became a pleaser to such an extreme that she developed health issues. She rarely said "no."

As long as Todd was leaning towards his responsible side and Benni was leaning towards her pleasing side, all went well. Their marriage looked good on the surface, but their relationship was paper-thin in terms of motivation and sustainability. When a crisis arose, their marriage immediately fell into serious trouble.

Todd developed an emotional connection with their babysitter. He found it flattering that a pretty, young teenager wanted to hang out and chat with him, even when she was off the clock. Todd was selfishly living out his lost teen years. The babysitter had her own emotional issues, causing her to seek the attention of a married man 10 years older. Benni noticed that the babysitter was hanging around too much. However, as a people pleaser, she did not share her concerns about what she was observing.

Todd got caught. His inappropriate actions and feelings were exposed. Although not illegal, his emotionally inappropriate actions threatened to ruin everything. Thankfully, accountability relationships surrounding Todd called him out, not only exposing his actions, but also helping him repair the damage he caused. Their marriage was held together by supportive friends and family who kept them accountable. Support got their fragile relationship through the crisis.

True guilt versus false guilt

Gaslighting is a form of manipulation that causes victims to doubt themselves. Michelle has been visiting my office for quite some time. A victim of gaslighting, she often feels guilty whether or not she should. Her husband Mike often uses gaslighting to manipulate Michelle. It messes with her head. For example, Mike has Sheltie dogs that howl incessantly. The howling at night affects Michelle's sleep. Michelle also owns a dog. One day, before running errands, Michelle asked Mike to take her dog outside to do his business while she was gone. Mike, contrary to Michelle's instructions, tied her pup to the front step throughout her absence. When Michelle arrived home and saw her dog tied in a hot sunny location, she got angry. Mike defended his actions with, "I thought maybe you wanted him to have some sun while you were out." In actuality, Mike was hiding his intentions about being angry with Michelle for getting upset when the Shelties howled. He disguises his anger by appearing supportive. Mike tells Michelle to be grateful for his gesture. But she is not. Mike's manipulative gesture concealed two perverse motives: to get even with Michelle for how she reacts when his dogs howl, and to evoke feelings of guilt for Michelle's ingratitude to Mike for caring for her dog, although maliciously, while she ran errands. Michelle second-guesses herself about being angry versus being grateful for Mike's effort to care for her dog.

Manipulative scheming also occurs when Mike cooks for the family, then digs for a compliment from Michelle on his cooking. He sows guilt when she does not compliment him even though he fails to compliment her cooking. Sometimes, Mike makes false accusations that Michelle rarely cooks, causing her to feel bad. Unfortunately, Mike does not care about how his gaslighting affects her. What Michelle struggles with is false guilt.

During her childhood, Michelle received consistent family messages that neither she nor her performance were good enough. She learned to blame herself for any problems in her relationships. She became a people pleaser. For example, Michelle felt bad her parents were in debt. She knew they spent money they did not have in order to pay for her extracurricular activities. She falsely believed it was her responsibility to pay off the debt in order to be thought of as a good daughter and thus win the approval of her family – a fruitless effort as it turned out to be. Conditioned to act out of feeling guilty, Michelle does so without thinking how unfair the situation is.

Influenced by her parents, Michelle followed a model of parenting portraying herself as the idyllic wife and mother responsible for the house, cooking and cleaning, all done with joy and enthusiasm. Based on her need to please, she never expected help, thanks, or respect for all she did. As a result, she enabled her husband and two sons to behave irresponsibly. False guilt says, "It is my fault if things don't get done in the home!" False guilt says, "I should not expect anyone to help me!" When Michelle understood how false guilt had affected her, and the shame of not feeling good enough had driven her, she became accountable for the state of her home. Progress ensued. Michelle is challenging her sons now. She is helping them to be more mindful of their attitudes and behaviors. She has been empowered to lead them as their mother, not to wait on them hand and foot. She is establishing her empowerment as a mother as she sorts through what is true guilt versus false guilt. Simple questions like, "Is that fair?" and "Is that balanced?" are making a difference.

Guilt is a forensic term. The word is actually more of a legal description than an emotion. Guilt is a statement of fact: "I made a mistake, I did something wrong, I am guilty even if I do not feel *guilty*." True guilt suggests that you are accurately described as having done something wrong.

False guilt is about the accompanying false feeling of wrongdoing. However, when I have done something wrong and feel bad about it, that is healthy. Dr. John Bradshaw labels that as "functional shame." False guilt occurs when nothing has been done wrong, but the bad feelings of wrong exist anyway. Some of those feelings of false guilt come from within (intrinsic) based on expectations, insecurity, previous wounding, or bad experiences. Other feelings of false guilt come from without (extrinsic). Extrinsic false guilt comes from other people's words, implied words and expectations, gestures, and projected shame. False guilt is a crippling influence, but it gets even worse when the emotion of shame moves beyond "I made a mistake" to "I am a mistake." Bradshaw labeled the latter as "toxic shame." It is frequently the root cause of substance abuse, addiction, self-harm, and a myriad of other negative behaviors.

The purpose of extrinsic false guilt is manipulation. When Michelle began to understand false guilt and manipulation, she realized she did not need to engage in activity or behavior driven by manipulation. We do not need to live under the burden of guilt. We can own our mistakes. We can correct our wrongdoing and poor behavior(s). We do not need to let others manipulate us by wielding false guilt.

Permission granting

Permission granting is about giving others permission to choose how they want to think and behave. Whether an individual engages in a conversation or not, that is their choice. When an individual walks away from an argument without resolving it, that is their decision. When an individual chooses not to cooperate, he cannot be forced. Ultimately, everyone decides whether to work together or independently, or whether to be in or out of a relationship. Unfortunately, some use manipulation and false guilt to force others to engage, cooperate, or relate. They may arrogantly believe their role is to manage others in the relationship: "If I don't remind her to pick up the groceries, then we will have no food in the house!"

Permission granting means I surrender my right to be in control. Rather than micro-managing others, we merely offer boundaries. We can ask questions to establish those boundaries or to understand the boundaries of others. Why do people have difficulty asking tough questions that establish boundaries? Perhaps they do not know what to do with the information! It helps to ask, "Can I get back to you on that?" It gives permission to individuals so they can think about it.

Relational permission

Most people are not content with giving others permission to choose unless they themselves are choosing. But in a relationship, what happens when the person's choice contravenes what I want? A person can offer a boundary like, "You can lie to me if you want, but I might catch you in that lie. Please know that if I catch you lying to me, I have the freedom to respond however I choose. I reserve the right to be upset with you." This response is better than the ultimatum technique: "If you ever lie to me, we're done!"

When we let go of trying to control each other, where the anger factor comes into relationships, we actually get better results, especially in building trust. When we allow each other freedom within healthy boundaries, we create mutual respect. By giving each other permission to choose how to live, we give each other the power to choose what we want as an outcome. Do you want to be close or distant? Do you want to be alone or intimate? Giving others permission and freedom pushes back on our need for control.

Personal permission

The person who is exploited or manipulated, a person with no boundaries, usually has difficulty saying no. People such as Carrie, in Chapter 3, failed to give herself permission to be treated respectfully. You have to give yourself permission first. When you stand up for yourself, ask questions like, "Would it be okay if I....?" as opposed to stubbornly stating, "I'm not going to..." or worse, being passive-aggressive in your actions. Often, a blind spot in these areas allows injustice. We do not see that we have enough value to be accepted until we cross the threshold of getting permission. Then, we will be treated with more respect.

Fear and permission

I encourage couples to give each other permission to choose how they want to relate or not relate. The outcome of how they relate will eventually become apparent. However, some individuals have a more difficult time relinquishing control in the relationship. Therefore, they refuse to give permission for others to make their own decisions. When individuals have not experienced a healthy relationship, they fear the outcome when they are not "in the know" or do not have an influence or control over a situation. Others might have a fear of being left out altogether. This need to know, to influence or to be in control can be for self-preservation, a need to feel connected, or a belief that no one can be trusted. Then, the typical reaction is to become more controlling about how the relationship develops. We desire to control what we do not know or cannot influence. However, the good news is that over time, the truth about the dynamics of a relationship comes to the surface.

Meanwhile, waiting for the garbage can to overflow while the husband experiences new-found freedom from nagging (chapter three), we see a new reality emerge. In those moments of developing new relationship skills, couples are encouraged to review the fundamentals of their relationship so as not to get lost in the details of the "what if?" questions. Everyone wants to be able to control the unknown. Inevitably, when one partner exerts control, the other gets upset.

It might not feel like it initially, but when push comes to shove, the permission to choose actually makes people more successful. Fear of letting go is part of the fear of the unknown. Spouses granting each other permission to express their true thoughts and feelings without reprisal or consequence is an expression of overcoming fear. It is integral to a healthy, empowered relationship. Granting permission says, "I trust you." Many criticize others without taking an honest look at themselves and what they need to change. When they realize what they personally need to change, they, in turn, empower others to change. Permission granting empowers change.

We only need to manage what we are responsible for, looking after and changing our own attitudes and actions as necessary, without worrying about others. It would be great if we could grant the people around us the permission to respond in healthy ways, rather than sharing our negativity, control, anxiety, or unhealthy shame. Thus, when I see a spouse not giving their partner freedom to choose, I ask, "So what? What if they don't do this? What will happen?"

If the goal is to improve communication, then we need to give each other room to choose to succeed or fail at the relationship. As the grip of control loosens, communication improves.

Trust: Who to trust?

Boundaries are important. However, there is a limit to the boundaries that can be applied. Not everything can be controlled or limited through boundaries. At some point you will have to exercise trust. Ask yourself, "Who do I trust if I let go of control in this relationship?" If you are a person of faith, the big picture suggests you have to trust God. If you are not a person of faith, it is a similar focus, a focus of trusting the principle, trusting that truth will surface.

We all have to establish and stick to principles, such as:

- Truth will surface
- Control doesn't help anyone
- Love wins
- When we work at this, we will achieve desired outcomes

- When we seek understanding, we'll eventually know the facts and the truth
- Everyone needs a measure of trust
- There are supporting behaviors that help build trust

Building trust requires closing the gap between the known and unknown. There is a perpetual gap between our desired outcome and our current reality. It is easy to fill that gap with fear, cynicism, judgment, and doubt. However, those defensive, self-preserving options of negativity do not improve our lives.

The challenge is to establish something better to fill the gap. Denial does not work; the gap must be filled with a positive remedy – that is, trust. Until we have behavior and accountability that matches it, we are just going to have to trust.

Balancing trust

Trust needs limits. Ultimately, broken trust has consequences. Trust begs the question of what I will do if trust is repeatedly broken. We all need to be respected. I will step back when being disrespected. Broken trust needs separation. It needs a time out. When trust is violated or broken, a new agreement needs to be reached. Professional counselling is often necessary.

Craig had been unfaithful to his wife on two occasions, three weeks apart. He was sincerely remorseful. Craig had acted out of anger towards his wife, Nancy, because she had lied to him. He was not very forgiving. Throughout their marriage, Nancy had a history of lying. Lying had eroded any trust they had in each other. Nancy had actually lied well before they were married. Craig had come to resent a marriage based on lies. Concerning the affair, both were at fault, but for different reasons. His share of the blame was more obvious because he cheated on Nancy. In response, Nancy compensated for his destructive behavior by running up over $30,000 of debt, mostly hidden credit card debts. Her lies continued, only making matters worse.

Two decades passed before Craig put forth an ultimatum: either Nancy would go for counselling or he would move out. The trust of keeping agreements to work on personal issues before working on relational issues had disintegrated. While attending counselling, however, Nancy only focused on surface issues, never sharing any information from her past or digging into the lies that preceded the marriage. The shallow relationship this couple did have was in part built on lies that Nancy refused to rectify. Her family history of sweeping it under the carpet created a culture of secrecy. She made no effort to own her personal baggage. Craig's anger only worsened.

Craig stayed true to his ultimatum. He kept his promise and left the house. It is an unfortunate outcome, but the unresolved lying from Nancy and her unforgiving choice to hide her overspending, along with Craig's decision to have an affair and now leave the house, ended the relationship. Craig believed that if he could create a tension that would cause Nancy to reconsider, they would have a chance to rebuild a trusting relationship. He never thought it would require such a drastic measure.

Assertive Questions

What are assertive questions?

Assertive questions can be used to achieve a desired outcome. They can be abrasive and challenging, and might even back someone into a corner, but they are effective. Assertive questions can become manipulative. However, when the motivation is pure, they transform into positive reinforcement. When a strong point needs to be made, or when a client holds a strong position, I use an assertive question.

Assertive questions work best when you mirror the behavior or statements of the individual with whom you are speaking. The assertive approach tends to neutralize strong dysfunction. When you use the other person's language, tone, or expressions to make your point, you will communicate assertively. Sometimes, speaking softly with gentle questions works, but there is a time and place for speaking assertively.

Assertive questions don't seek to escalate the situation. They thwart repeated stubbornness or inflexibility. They match strength with strength. They may seem offensive, but they move the dialogue towards confrontation by using the opponent's language.

For example, a morning rush and a messy bathroom conflict could start with a simple question like, "Are you going to clean up before you go?" The question is simple enough, but the partner could get defensive and respond, "You have no idea how important this appointment is." If not cleaning up is a one-time event, it is not an appropriate time for an assertive question. However, when it has happened consistently, it would be fair to respond (perhaps later in the day after the big meeting), "Did we not agree to clean up after ourselves before we left in the morning?"

Managing assertive questions

The effectiveness of assertive questions is very evident in the area of forgiveness. When people have a perception that they should be forgiven but refuse to forgive others, it is appropriate to ask assertive questions such as, "What is fair about that? Why should you be forgiven but not them?"

It is my observation that generally, in marriage, husbands will be quicker to forgive. Wives will often think, "I can't forgive him until I can trust him." Dozens of women have admitted such thoughts in our sessions. My response is an assertive question: "So, how is that fair?" The question causes them to consider separating forgiveness and trust. She needs to suspend her issue with trust so she can deal with her unforgiveness. Trust and forgiveness are two separate issues.

Clay, in chapter 6, completely understood when I would challenge him with the word "fair." For Fran, it was the word "justice." Fran was not looking for what was fair or equal; she sought the big picture, the process that would lead to justice.

I find these words bring accountability because they allow individuals to see themselves as they really are. It is an assertive strategy, not a defensive posture. These questions take us tactically into the battle plan as opposed to being more combative or picking a fight. They need to be used with wisdom and discretion. When we do not know our audience, it can quickly go sideways. Confrontations using assertive questions do not always go as planned. However, when things are escalated, wisely wielded assertive questions effectively resolve differences.

The progression of questions

Questions follow a natural progression. Starting with general questions, we move to specific and emotional questions, then we hit the target with the ultimate questions. The closer we get to the core, the more powerful, more personal, and more targeted the questions become.

When you first walk into an automotive dealership, the salesman might ask you if you are in the market for a car, a van, a truck, or an SUV. If you say, "A car!" his next question might be about size, then the number of doors, then color, followed by what options you want. These are all general questions, shallow in nature. Specific questions might include, "What brings you to our dealership? Do you like our brand of vehicles? Is there a reason you are looking for a new car?" Ultimate questions would be, "Do you need financing? Are you ready to sign on the dotted line?"

A great salesman should be able to get you to the ultimate question in a matter of minutes because he wants a sale. In relationships, because it takes time to explore thoughts and feelings, it could take several weeks to get to an ultimate question.

Depending on the events that lead into what is happening, you can sometimes jump right into direct, ultimate questions, while other times you need to take time. For example, when a spouse feels upset, it is not appropriate to tell them to get over it or to ask, "Why don't you do something about your attitude?" Rather, it would be more respectful to begin by asking indirect questions, then questions about the facts, followed by questions about opinions, then feelings. You could start by asking about context: "How was your day?" Initially, you just want insight into what they are thinking. Then you can ask, "What do you think happened to cause such a problem?" Next, gently move into the emotional arena. You ask them to share more openly about their opinions. "Why do you think that happened?" Then, specifically, you ask about feelings, "How do you feel about what happened?" then, more specifically, "Have you considered what you might do to solve that problem? Would you be willing to try something else? What are some other things you could try?" As you practice moving from general to specific kinds of questions, you create a safer, more engaging context for the relationship to develop.

Chapter 11

Where are the questions going?

"Transformation is a process, and as life
happens there are tons of ups and downs.
It's a journey of discovery - there are
moments on mountaintops and moments
in deep valleys of despair."
– Rick Warren

Contrast: Process versus outcome

In the quest for wholeness, it is important that we differentiate between process and outcome. Many couples come to counselling hoping that one or two sessions will get things fixed up quickly. It would be great to be able to wave a magic wand or to speak an encouraging comment that would make an instant difference and achieve their desired outcome of relational connectedness. It would be great if families could immediately reach the goal of family peace and harmony. Those desired *outcomes* are good, but it takes a *process* to get there.

In chapters seven and eight, we discussed several defense mechanisms and emotions that can create barriers to relationships. In that context, I told the story of a gentleman who discovered that he had difficulty with a "poor me" perspective and how he worked hard to overcome it. In a similar story, Vince had an equally difficult time with this perspective.

Vince is married to Olivia, the second marriage for both of them. Vince has children from his first marriage. He carries a great deal of shame because of the effect the divorce has had on his children. Vince feels bad that his children have to be shuttled between himself and his ex-wife, the frustrating "week on, week off" kind of relationship between dad and mom. He feels he has caused irreparable damage and instability to them. The source of his shame is believing that he is a bad father. Vince always contends to be the best dad on the planet to compensate for disappointing, inconveniencing, and hurting his children. In his thinking, this is all his fault; he believes he should have tried harder. We all tend to compensate when there are areas of our lives where we feel there is a shortfall.

During their engagement, Olivia often felt displaced during the children's week with Vince. She wanted

Vince's attention just like his children did. In fact, Vince and Olivia broke up for a period before their wedding because Vince favored his children to a fault. He and his kids were somewhat codependent, perhaps enmeshed. Vince constantly sided with his kids, expecting his future wife to accept it. He saw his children as innocent victims. In his self-pity, Vince felt himself to be a victim of Olivia because she did not accept his "victim children" attitude. How could their relationship survive when most of the people in the house are perceived victims?

Because shame produces fear, Vince functioned defensively. Whatever Olivia said during a conflict, Vince considered as criticism. Because his primary motivation was the well-being of his kids, Vince believed he could never be wrong. According to Olivia, she insisted that Vince would also have difficulty when others did not accept his ideas or values. Vince's need for acceptance was so great that, in order for Vince to feel accepted by his children, he believed he had to make them feel good and accepted. There was no opportunity for Olivia to openly discuss anything about Vince and his children. The subject was always off limits. Vince was never wrong in loving and caring for his kids. He protected them at the emotional expense of his fiancée.

After Vince and Olivia eventually married, Vince would often get angry with Olivia because he thought she could not accept him or how he cared for his children. Olivia was angry because she had no input in the situation.

She ended up alienating herself. By trying to change the dynamics of the relationship, she was reinforcing a wall of division with her frustration.

Both Vince and his kids were victimized by Olivia's anger, which became one more thing he needed to protect his children from. In Vince's thinking, most of his value and self-esteem was placed on how well his children were doing. To untangle these problems, we needed to help Vince understand Olivia's anger and what she needed to feel valued. In one conflict resolution conversation, the script went as follows:

"We're having this conflict because I want a new family tradition for my children, but Olivia won't go along with it," Vince said.

"What will it look like?" Olivia asked. "What's the purpose? What if I don't feel comfortable with it?" These are good questions, but they do not deal with her feelings of unfairness. Vince then stonewalled in silence.

"I don't feel comfortable with this!" Olivia said.

Vince then starts to manipulate the conversation. "You're seeing it all wrong!" he says. "You're only thinking of yourself. Can't you care about my kids too?"

"What?" Olivia responds. "I do care about them! I'm just asking about what our new family tradition will look like?

What are the reasons behind it? Is that too much to ask? Never mind. Never mind. I can't reason with you."

The conversations end because Olivia can't handle it when Vince starts to distort the issue by blaming her for the children's problems. It used to make her angry. When she tried to confront his blaming, Vince only got angrier, so now she just backs out of conversations completely. She then decided to establish conversational boundaries. She would simply back out of those conversations as he began to gaslight and cause Olivia to doubt herself and her perceptions of the situations Vince would reference. She decided to let him resolve the situation with his children.

In his mind, Vince only acted for the good of everybody involved. His thinking was, "I'm very good at caring for everybody else. Why can't you cut me some slack? Why can't you care about what I think is good?" Vince was constantly missing the main point: to work as a team with his new wife. His priorities for the relationship were distorted due to the shame he felt about the joint custody situation. This is where some hard questions were posed: Could he appreciate the huge sacrifices she had made for him, even before she married him? Could he see how Olivia had covered bases for him and his children when she stayed home to look after them during visitation weeks while Vince was at work? His children didn't have to go to daycare because Olivia stayed home to watch them. Could Vince see how unreasonable it was to be asking his wife to feel sorry for him when he felt he had to constantly prioritize his children, even over Olivia's feelings?

Vince was not being understanding at all. How could he *get* understanding? Ironically, the strategy that worked was for us to first push back on Olivia's anger. Because Olivia so desperately wanted a positive outcome, she was deeply committed to this process in spite of the fact that Vince had the glaring issues. They needed some new boundaries. In this instance, we could only change how Olivia engaged Vince in conversation.

Our process sought to determine what was "right" and "fair." First, Olivia needed to have peace with the process. Unfortunately, her search for fairness would take longer than she hoped, and would not achieve the outcome she desired. She had to give Vince permission to succeed or fail in their relationship, and to allow the process to unfold instead of insisting on her desire for an immediate outcome. Some people are driven by process while others are driven by outcome. Up until this point, Olivia was entirely focused on the outcome. As she became more committed to the process, she gave Vince some room and stopped being angry at every unjust and unfair thing he did. She stopped trying to change Vince. By simply granting him permission as well as establishing boundaries around what she should have to put up with regarding Vince's negative behaviors, things finally started changing. Vince, having the room to make mistakes all on his own, without Olivia trying to fix and correct his parenting, became fully aware of his "poor me" attitude. The more he monitored his attitude, the more open he was to doing things differently. Trust began to grow again.

Another couple, Logan and Lauren, needed help for a family situation. She could not tolerate how he related to their kids. He grew up in an aggressive home where the commands of the parents were to be heeded and immediately fulfilled – it was all about the outcome. Conversely, Lauren came from a family where there was more functional dialogue – no yelling, no mocking. Her family would talk things out and get things done as a *process*.

Logan wanted Lauren to support his method of parenting; he believed she should just go along with it. Lauren could not support him because she found his approach too harsh. As they sat in my office, we sorted through all their concerns. Logan finally realized how different Lauren's style of parenting and communicating was from his own. He could see the differences in family background but could not appreciate the process. He wanted to see immediate results. That was his focus. For him, it was all about tasks, performance, and getting it done. It was all about the outcome.

Logan and Lauren needed to agree on how to communicate in a way that was not so harsh and potentially destructive. Agreements need a way and a means, as a process takes time to understand. Most would agree, we all want family values and standards that include cooperation, effort, and respect. But Logan had difficulty understanding that if he would only change his aggressive behaviors and communication style, altering the parenting process, Lauren would be fully engaged and supportive of the values he was trying to instill and uphold. Logan's reasoning was, "As long as the outcome is in place, then why does the process even matter?" The challenge was to get Logan to look at himself and his methods and to realize the importance of process which builds relationships. The more assured he is of Lauren's support of achieving his desired outcomes, the more committed he is to put in the effort and necessary time required to create the process. This was a significant shift. Numerous obstacles could affect the process, so they needed to anticipate the roadblocks and stick with the process.

We need to anticipate that the path away from conflict may not go smoothly. When feelings are involved, things might not go according to plan. Feelings can and often do interfere with the process. It is not easy work to stay on task and be committed to the process, but it is necessary to reach the desired outcomes.

Process

Process involves action. Process brings change that is clearly moving in a determined manner and direction.

Process is the journey part of relationship – the part that involves emotion and how we feel as we head towards the outcome. Further, "process people" ensure all I's are dotted and T's are crossed; they often have the administrative skills in the relationship. In my experience, women seem to be more process oriented than men. Finally, process is the unfolding narrative of the ongoing story of the relationship.

Outcome

Outcome is the final result, or the completion. In the thinking process, outcome is the conclusion. Outcome-oriented people just want results; they crave the solution and focus on getting the job done. However, for those with an outcome bias, process can be tedious and frustrating.

In my opinion, outcome people are often referred to as task-oriented or results-oriented. On the other hand, processors use feelings to sense things. They want to consult everyone involved to be sure there is agreement so that everyone is happy. Processors are less concerned about systems; they would rather take their time and proceed carefully without being rushed. A common statement you might hear a processor say is, "I'm still thinking about it."

Outcome-oriented people often arrive at decisions faster because they tend to be driven to get things moving. They may not have thought through every option, but they are determined to deal with the immediate. They want to identify the salient factors that require immediate consideration because they base the outcome on raw data rather than overall data. For them, the goal is not about getting the answer that everyone accepts and respects. They are often accused of being unfeeling, cold, or careless.

The following academic sources provide more nuggets of understanding in this area.

In a thesis written by Karima Merchant entitled, "How Men And Women Differ: Gender Differences in Communication Styles, Influence Tactics, and Leadership Styles," applicable literature on this topic is reviewed.[14] Merchant found consistency among various authors and concluded from her research that men and women communicate in vastly different ways, stemming from unique views on the purpose of conversation.

I concur with Merchant's findings. She gives many examples of the differences between men and women. Women, for example, want to be at peace with one another and help one another. They desire cooperation. Consequently, they view conversation as a tool to selflessly connect, so they build relationships to achieve that end. Conversely, Merchant suggests that men utilize conversation to express their dominance and ability to problem solve. For them, conversation carries more of a utilitarian component in an effort to find solutions. She suggests that men avoid feelings or personal issues by focusing instead on what needs to be fixed.

Merchant concludes that women focus their conversation on others and their feelings by living in unity and harmony. The process of communication bears more importance when the goal is connection. Specific problem-solving outcomes are less important to women. Ultimately, the most valuable outcome of conversation for women, as Merchant finds, is the relationship created through the talking.

Merchant cites author John Gray, the author of *Men are from Mars, Women are from Venus*, who reached a similar conclusion, saying that men have an obvious purpose in conversation: to achieve results. Women, on the other hand, focus on the relationship itself more than results. They build a measure of their sense of self, based on feelings and on how well they perceive the relationship is going. Women, by stark contrast, look for the man to listen deeply and show caring, understanding, and empathy. The worst thing a man can do according a woman is to give unsolicited advice. But, that is generally the default behavior for men, the perpetual "fixers."[15]

Essentially, because males and females approach conversation so uniquely, this creates a divide in their communication, even before any words are exchanged. Their philosophy of conversation is diametrically opposed.

Merchant also makes reference to Deborah Tannen, author of *You Just Don't Understand: Women and Men in Conversation.* Tannen argues that in styles of conversation, women share their problems with each other to foster intimacy in relationship. To their continued disappointment, women expect men to reciprocate, sharing openly their problems, emotions, and feelings. However, when men hear women sharing their problems, their tendency is to immediately want to fix the issues; they become problem-solvers who suggest solutions. Merchant reiterates that Tannen's observations reflect the huge chasm between genders in their approach to conversation. Men are about outcomes; women are about the process of communication.[16]

Lauren and Logan reflect many of these gender-typical mannerisms. They faced a lot of conflict over what Logan points to as their kids' misbehavior. Lauren, a processor, wants to take time to make sure all appropriate factors are considered. Logan says of Lauren, "You're not supporting me. You don't say anything. When the kids are misbehaving, I look to you for support, but you don't say a word."

He wants her support in everything he does. He feels he gets no support at all from his wife. Lauren does not support Logan's desired outcome because she does not like the way he goes about getting her or the kids to support his desired outcome. She does not like his process. She would like more discussion on the approach, the associated problems, and the emotions involved. When Logan says to the kids, "You will agree with this, you will do this, and you will like it," Lauren labels it as bullying. She wants the kids to be treated with more respect. She wants their input and to care for their feelings. It is her way of saying to Logan, "You need to fix the process here, not just achieve an outcome!" To her, the conversation has great intrinsic value.

After spending considerable time to achieve a working agreement between Lauren and Logan, my question was, "Can we come up with something where the outcome is agreeable *and* at the same time take a look at the *process* to get there?" Many times, Logan and Lauren were so polarized between process and outcome they couldn't see the forest for the trees. Logan was willing to look at the process, but would he know how to follow the process? Not unless he could follow a step-by-step set of instructions to function well in the process. Lauren needs to come back to the agreement that she has to continually ask Logan the questions that will help him focus on the process, as opposed to only looking at the outcome.

Chapter 12

Skills development

"Every artist was first an amateur."
– Ralph Waldo Emerson

Improved communication is an essential component in working towards a greater quality of relationships and life, and we all need to learn to improve the quality of our communication.

The power of asking for permission

I have worked with individuals who struggle with physical pain management. Physicians and physiotherapists working in this field have discovered the power of asking permission, as patients deal with their pain. This is important because individuals who are experiencing pain also have related anxieties. They anticipate the worst, and this elevates functions in the body to prepare for the worst. In order to manage their pain, the individual learns to anticipate what might cause increased pain. Knowing what to avoid is a good pain management technique, unless what is anticipated is unrealistic.

When assessing a patient's pain, medical professionals ask for permission to touch the painful area, or to talk about it. A certain degree of pain can be created or mitigated by anxiety and fear in some pain-related issues. The brain anticipates threats to the painful area and prepares to defend against the intrusion. It has been found that when the patient becomes involved in the assessment or treatment, their anxiety decreases, and the level of pain is correspondingly lowered. Therefore, asking permission gives the patient control over the situation as well as understanding about what is going to occur as the professional proceeds.

Asking for permission to proceed should always take precedence when engaging another individual, especially when there is the potential of evoking a defensive reaction. Contemplating a request is a matter of personal consideration. When the request remains unclear, the contemplator can respond with "maybe."

The power of maybe

I have experienced that men generally tend to be slower than women when processing emotional information or cues. Consequently, a lot of men become defensive when they communicate in the context of a relationship. In my office, I frequently witness guys shutting down emotionally when they are uncertain as to how to respond, especially in an emotionally charged situation. Those who shut down usually think no one can challenge them when they are not talking, so they stonewall. They believe aggressive communicators will eventually talk themselves out. They might even think, "If I don't agree or disagree, I'm in a better position and less likely to get in trouble." So, men learn to say "maybe" as a safety net. Saying "maybe" or "I am not sure" may be perceived as cowardly, but it buys time to think. Instead of getting defensive, consider the word "maybe" as an opportunity for a timeout.

Getting more time to process is a huge win. "Maybe" can remove the defensive position people normally take when they feel unsure, blindsided, or under attack. Defensiveness creates or further escalates a conflict. It's never good to agree to what causes you uncertainty, nor to defend anything that is unclear. It is better to leave an issue unresolved than to engage in a potentially destructive conversation. When you do not know what you think or feel about a situation, leave it at "maybe" or "I am not sure" and think about it. Resist the pressure to respond or react.

"Maybe" allows you a time of respite so you can take a break to think, to form an answer or another question clearly, without the pressure of an emotionally heightened situation. Unlike "yes" or "no," the word "maybe" is noncommittal, nonconclusive, and nonthreatening. It offers a touch of agreement without the threat of relational tension or unwanted verbal exchanges. It eliminates the pressure to finalize or to draw conclusions. More importantly, "maybe" removes the potential for disagreement, offering a win-win situation. It offers some resolution without combative or defensive behaviors, leaving the door open to process an incomplete discussion sometime in the future.

On the flip side, "maybe" can be interpreted as a "no." So, in good faith, the one who says "maybe" will need to eventually follow up with a definitive "yes" or "no." Do not ignore the issue; return after a reasonable time of consideration.

The grace given to think about it does not last forever. "Think about it" is a phrase which says the point is important, worth considering, and will not be dismissed. You want time to develop a reasonable and intelligent response. Thoughtful consideration is fair, and both sides win.

The power of forgiveness

When you resent something said or done and are not able to forgive, you will remain stuck on the issue you resent. Resentment creates a chasm of distrust. Therefore, you will find it increasingly more difficult to converse with someone you don't trust. Regardless of whom you resent (a spouse, friend, employer, family member, etc.), your feelings of resentment will become a barrier in that relationship.

Don is a good guy who is committed to his wife, family, friends, and career. As a pastor, he has given his life to church ministry, aspiring to make the world a better place. However, in recent years, struggling with the politics of the church community, he has begun to use occasional sarcasm to alleviate his frustrations. Sarcasm has changed his pattern of behavior. Like many pastors I have worked with over the years, Don struggled to meet the needs of his congregants when navigating their diverse opinions. For example, one member considered Don's sermons too long, while another believed they were not long enough. The music was too loud for some and not loud enough for others.

Don had begun to resent the church complainers. However, he was not just a victim of his situation at church. The most difficult problem he had to manage was the assault suffered by his daughter. She struggled with PTSD for several years following a horrible crime that took place at the hands of an angry young man.

There was nothing Don could do about the culprit who had brought enormous pain into his family. The young man was never charged, never tried. Don carried deep, painful anger in his heart, and bitterness towards the assailant. Only the sting of unforgiveness remained. Don told me about a violent dream he had in which he attacked his daughter's assailant with a baseball bat. He awoke tormented with thoughts of hatred and vengeance.

After sorting through his varied emotions, I asked, "When are you going to forgive?" He later told me that my question was life-changing for him. He knew all about forgiveness, had preached on the steps of forgiveness, and helped others understand how to know that they have really been forgiven. However, as knowledgeable as he was on the topic, Don had yet to forgive his daughter's assailant. In the process, Don realized that forgiveness was needed for himself. By forgiving the assailant, Don could be freed from his anger and resentment.

Don committed to process his anger through complete forgiveness. He wrote a letter to the assailant, which I later read. The letter was seething, brutally honest, and toxic as Don purged his soul of the tension and poison he had suppressed for months. Don never mailed the letter. That was not the point. The letter was a method for Don to detox his emotions. He wrote it again and again until he had gotten out every negative thought. When he could finally stop hating the man who had hurt his family, he felt free.

Forgiveness was about Don getting his heart and mind right. He had been tormented and held in bondage by emotional shackles before he forgave the assailant. Forgiveness changed his life. With the toxins gone, he was able to move on.

After decades of clinical practice, I have heard many different versions of Don's story. Some are stories of hurt and anger, while others are of shame or high anxiety. Often, family-of-origin dysfunction results in resentment that burdens most people. Some suppress resentment for their entire lives. But those who choose to forgive begin loving themselves and others.

Whether PTSD, grief, shame, anger, stress, or abuse, I believe forgiveness must be a part of the healing process. Unfortunately, most fail to realize that forgiveness is for them and not just the one who hurt them. Consequently, in seeking justice, retribution, or revenge, they do not recognize the damage that anger inflicts on themselves and their relationships.

How different genders handle forgiveness

According to both academic sources and my clinical observations, men and women handle forgiveness differently. For men, forgiveness means, "I did something wrong. I'm sorry. Forgive me." End of story. In most cases, men tend to be quicker to own the damage when they realize what they have done. Through acknowledging their shortcomings and mistakes, men want to move on towards "fixing it."

For women, on the other hand, I have observed that forgiveness is about a violation of trust. "Yes, you made a mistake, but now I don't trust you. Therefore, I can't forgive you. You have to behave in a way that helps me to believe that it won't happen again. Then I can trust you. Then I can forgive you". Women need to *feel* the trust because forgiveness alone does not repair the feeling of distrust. That feeling must be settled in order for trust to be reestablished. Therefore, when the offender is proven trustworthy, they will forgive. Generally speaking, women need freedom from a feeling of distrust.

The hard truth about forgiveness

Trust is about reconciliation. Reconciliation is about working out differences between individuals. Obviously, restoring and re-establishing trust takes time. You cannot effectively rebuild something as sacred as trust in a 10-minute conversation. I believe forgiveness is essential. Unforgiveness must be personally and individually resolved before you can reconcile any differences in a relationship.

From self-care to serving others

Before you take off on a commercial airline, the flight attendant demonstrates how to work a seatbelt. They will also point out the emergency exits. Finally, they instruct you about how important it is to be "selfish" when it comes to use of the oxygen mask. They remind parents travelling with young children to put on their own oxygen mask first, then assist their children. The point is that it is hard to assist or serve a child if you are unconscious. The lesson from this: self-care first, then service.

Self-care can easily be neglected by not forgiving others. We become hurting victims when we chose not to forgive, and we only hurt ourselves. Forgiving others is one way I can look after myself. If I forgive, I am demonstrating a profound level of self-care because forgiveness is a decision. It is not something you need to wait on for all the right conditions to align, attitudes to adjust, or circumstances to become favorable.

Just to be clear, the conditions will never be perfect to forgive. If you are holding on with great hopes and anticipation, waiting for an apology first, waiting for a person to change or to show evidence of remorse, you will likely experience tremendous disappointment. To not forgive is to only hurt yourself, to be held hostage to events and behaviors in others that you are powerless to change or control. You *can*, however, control your choice to forgive or not. You can choose to take care of yourself. You can choose to change the part you can control by working on your end first (forgiveness) and then working on the relationship later (reconciliation). You can deal with your own stuff and leave others to their own issues. You can work at freeing yourself from the entanglement of unforgiveness and resentment.

I have a saying: "You can't resolve what you still resent." I do not want to be one who resents, as I believe resentment comes with a cost. I want to be the kind of person who forgives.

One of my clients was a man named Mason. His wife, Evelyn, was well aware that Mason was more focused on work than their marriage. He was committed to his marriage, but more so to the idea of marriage. I would not say he was deeply in love with his wife. He was a career man. Evelyn was coping. I met with her and Mason in couples counselling. She was encouraged to confront Mason on some of their glaring marriage issues, but she never did. When Evelyn did not confront him on his issues, I confronted him with a rather strong boundary, but recognizing his shame, I affirmed him, spoke of my support of him as an individual, and told him that I cared enough to work on his difficult issues with him. Mason was interested in resolving his shame and anger issues. Much of his anger was tied into his struggle to forgive others. Previously, against the advice of Evelyn, Mason had bought into a partnership in a new business. It became a crushing and humbling venture for him when his partner embezzled all the money. Evelyn was patient in that season and did not take an "I told you so" posture. She was caring and supportive enough to attend counselling and support Mason as he processed unresolved resentments – even if it included her.

I assigned Mason to read a couple of books on forgiveness. The books reinforced what we had been discussing and helped Mason to more deeply understand forgiveness. It also helped him to realize how angry he really was and how unforgiving he had been towards himself and others. Mason also realized the cost of unforgiveness and how much he needed to be forgiven for some of his actions toward others. The impact of forgiveness coupled with his wife's understanding broke the back of Mason's stubborn resistance to letting go of his resentments.

I have seen much smaller business losses destroy marriages, but because Mason and Evelyn worked through the issues, they stayed together. Today, Mason is a different man. He has gradually learned to forgive others and has softened towards Evelyn. I asked him if he had ever thought about how he could serve her. In other words, rather than putting himself first, could he learn to honor and respect her? After all, she had been incredibly patient with him when he had invested and lost so much in the business.

Mason told me Evelyn wanted to travel. I challenged him to think about her request as an area where he could love and serve her practically. Mason thought about my challenge and considered how he could put her first. At their next appointment, Mason committed to the challenge to serve. It was one of several gestures that really helped their marriage.

Because Mason had learned not to be so angry and resentful, he became open to doing things differently. He used to get terribly defensive when being confronted, but has become more teachable. His terrible business experience helped to open his eyes to his imperfections. He has continued to grow in kindness and humility, loving, and caring more for his wife.

A year later, Mason tried to sell the business but it would not sell. It was a struggle for him to not get top dollar for something into which he had invested colossal amounts of time and resources. I asked him if he would be okay with losing some money on the sale, essentially a "So what?" question he was not able to handle a year earlier. He said he could live with that. Now that Mason was functioning in a new paradigm of forgiveness – less angry and more emotionally developed – he could let things go. It was good to see him coming to terms with the ambition, pride, and intensity that had hurt his marriage earlier. Now he was emotionally and mentally capable of letting go of disappointments because he learned how to process disappointments through forgiveness. Someone eventually bought the business for a good price, and it all worked out well. He had been willing to let his stubbornness take a hit. That would not have been the case in previous years. As he learned to forgive, many areas of his life and marriage began to heal.

As Mason increased in humility, let go of his pride and anger, and stopped being stubborn, a change happened in him. Helping Mason through a long journey to wholeness has encouraged me to ask other clients, "What are you holding on to?" I found that whatever it is - when clients just can't let go, when they cannot forgive, when they cannot stop being angry, when they cannot trust, or when they choose resentment or cynicism - they are presenting indicators of a lack of healing, a deficiency in wholeness.

Years ago, I was consulting with a company that had a complicated history. There were several transitions and some new staff, one of whom was an employee who made some professional mistakes and took money from the organization. In the chaos, staff became disillusioned by the company standards and practices. Eventually, there was a company split. When the dust settled, the original owner of the company took half of his staff with him to start over in the building right next door. My assessment was that after the founding director had stepped down, the next CEO had mismanaged the affairs of the company and had done things that were inappropriate and unethical. He was fired. The subsequent CEO had previously been running the operations when the founding director abandoned the organization. This new CEO had not been treated particularly well in the process and, subsequently, had difficulty in reconciling the transition and move of the founding director. Because of the proximity of the new company, the new CEO would often run in to the founding director, which became awkward and offensive. It was a reminder of all the hurtful things that had happened at the time of his departure. It weighed on him even though he knew better, so he made a conscious choice to forgive. Every day for three months, he intentionally made the choice to forgive and not let his internal dialogue get the better of him.

During those three months, something changed in the heart of the new CEO. He realized that he had been thoroughly healed in his heart when he heard news that the founding director and their staff were facing a difficult situation. Rather than being cynically happy for their situation, the new CEO discovered he had truly forgiven them because he felt compassion toward them, not malice. It felt good to know he had forgiven them, and that he no longer judged them for the mistakes they had made. He was actually able to serve them by offering to help them deal with their situation.

A year later, the founding director of the company approached the CEO to ask forgiveness for how they had conducted themselves in the situation, how they had mishandled the unresolved issues stemming from the previous CEO, and how they had taken their anger out on the new CEO. The new CEO was able to look them in the eye and, with no vindictiveness, say with full sincerity, "You are forgiven already." That was the end of the conversation. He had already worked it out and reconciled it in his heart. When the day of apology and reconciliation finally came, he did not need it. He had not waited for the perfect conditions. He forgave first. He was at peace. He had moved on. The forgiveness was his piece to manage and he did it without needing an apology from the founding director.

What are you angry at? Why are you angry? A helpful exercise is to make a list about the things that you are angry about and to ask yourself, "What do I need to forgive?" and "What do I need to reconcile?" It is even more extraordinary to forgive people before you reconcile. It is a potentially liberating part of our lives to be able to come together with people with whom we had our differences, to see beyond conflict, to love and care for those who have hurt us, to release them, and to not hold our feelings over their heads.

Reconciliation, not perfection

As we reconcile, it does not mean that everything is perfect. The negotiation of reconciliation rarely leaves both sides totally satisfied. The important thing is that we forgive and carry on. For example, the 88th season of the National Hockey League (NHL) did not see a single game played. The collective bargaining agreement between the team owners and the players had expired in the early summer of 2005. Negotiations broke down that summer and continued through the fall. Players were locked out of the arenas. No games were played through the winter and spring of 2006.

When the same situation occurred in the fall of 2012, there were many delays and it appeared the season would be cancelled once again. A few days into the new year, suddenly it was "Game on!" An agreement had been reached. The fact that there was a new agreement in place did not mean that both sides got what they wanted, nor did it mean that both sides were particularly happy. In fact, it had been stated that neither the owners or players were happy with the new collective bargaining agreement, but it was enough of an agreement to work. In the end, everyone was tired of the stalemate and had prepared to lose or give up something in order to move on. Under the new terms of agreement, the owners and players reconciled enough of their differences to agree to play the game of hockey. That is reconciliation.

The power of fairness

I hear a recurring refrain in my office: "It's not fair!" Hardly a week goes by that someone doesn't say these words. The problem is this statement is terribly true. Life is not fair. Nor are work, school, or relationships fair. Pretty much anything you can think of is not fair. Often in our relationships, there is imbalance in what is considered to be fair. We try to compensate in our pursuit of fairness, doing whatever we can to not come up with the wrong end of the proverbial stick.

We all know, generally speaking, that men and women often communicate differently. When the "life is not fair" perspective is used in a manipulative manner, I sometimes need to interject a question such as, "What's not fair about that?" or "What should 'fair' or 'fairness' look like in this situation?" That question makes an impact in that it can create conflict, clarification, or awareness. It is often a way of dealing with manipulative challenges from either gender. For example, when a spouse makes a remark about their partner's behavior(s) stating that it is not fair that he or she does this or that, I might ask, "What *is* unfair about it?" As they process that question, I try to listen to hear some of their terms, phrases, or words to reflect back to them.

Essentially, this is a tool to guide the conversation. It leads into individuals having to deal with their own perspectives rather than making it about everybody else or somebody else, usually the injustices they perceive of their spouse's life. Ultimately, it is not about what is fair or not, but rather, what leads us all into a place where we are processing the issues of our own hearts, our anger, our fear, our shame, and whatever unpleasant emotion is creating a conflict. The issue is not as much about our circumstances as it is about our thoughts, our reactions, our emotions, our actions, and taking the right steps to process those thoughts and feelings, to work through them, to move on with forgiveness, grace, and a positive attitude. We all have pain and problems. We make choices about rehearsing, cursing, or nursing our past. Questions help us to reverse negative thoughts by challenging the downward spiral and moving on towards a more positive resolution.

Are we prepared to ask the questions that will take us to a place of reconciliation? What are we prepared to make negotiable for the sake of reconciliation? Happiness is nice, but are we willing to put our own happiness aside to be able to forgive others? These are tough questions. We need to find a balance between being a passive pushover and fighting for our own way. Happiness does not come when everything goes our own way; that is selfishness. There is, however, a sense of peace that comes when we forgive, whether others have apologized or not.

The power of boundaries

Our earlier comments on parameters have already opened the discussion on the topic of boundaries and control. The word "control" can have a very negative connotation, especially when used in terms of manipulative control. However, control can be a good thing. You want control if your car is on an icy slope heading towards a busy, crowded intersection, for example. None of us wish to be "controlling" (manipulating) or "controlled" (manipulated) in a relationship, but we do want a sense of having clear boundaries and the ability to determine our own course.

Dr. Henry Cloud and Dr. John Townsend, both clinical psychologists, have written the benchmark, definitive work on boundaries entitled *Boundaries: When to Say Yes, When to Say No to Take Control of Your Life*. They help us to understand "boundaries" as the contemporary psychological term that is rooted in the geo-political concept of a simple property line. Boundaries help us determine what responsibilities are ours and what another's responsibilities are another's to own and manage.[17]

Cloud and Townsend discuss the formulation of boundaries in childhood development, and the importance for children to be permitted and encouraged to say "no." They suggest that the word "no" is a powerful word in establishing and maintaining proper and healthy boundaries. The authors also talk about boundaries in different adult contexts, such as demanding bosses, disagreeable spouses, controlling church leaders, and parents. They tell a story of a young couple where the husband's meddling parents do not respect the societal norms of appropriate distance or boundaries. The couple is not enabled to emerge in healthy marital, relational function until they establish boundaries with the parents. I have seen dozens of clients with exactly the same issue where they have to establish strong boundaries with their parents so they can mature and develop families of their own.

Cloud and Townsend want their readers to take responsibility and establish boundaries in order to stand up for themselves against being disrespected, bullied, or controlled by others. A lack of good boundaries can lead to anger, frustration, an overwhelming sense of obligation, burnout, relationship problems, and emotional problems such as depression and anxiety. If you struggle to establish healthy boundaries, either because you feel the need to control others or feel you are being controlled by others, I would encourage you to read the book.

Questions are a powerful tool to establish clear and strong boundaries. A question is a neutral means of quickly and gently establishing boundaries. For example, if you see a manager bullying a co-worker in your office, you could step in and calmly and respectfully ask, "Sir, do you think that loud tone of voice and name-calling is appropriate?"

Of course, it is not appropriate for a manager to yell at anyone or call anyone names. Without the use of questions, you may inappropriately make judgmental statements such as, "You are a disrespectful boss!" which often makes things even worse. Or, you might escalate the situation if you blurt out, "Stop that! That's mean!" You may infuriate your boss if you say, "That is *not* how to manage. I don't want to *ever* hear you call him a jerk again!" That is establishing a boundary, but the boundary might end up with you being fired. Although the above statements may be true, a question from a more neutral posture, often creates a healthy boundary by bringing a person to a place of thought, "Is it appropriate? Maybe not! What are my options? How can I rectify this situation?"

Who needs boundaries?

<u>Jenny</u>

Jenny needed boundaries. She liked to think of herself as pragmatic. However, her pragmatism came across as "blunt opinion" rather than what she called "practical outspokenness." Consistently alienating others, she did not have many close friends. It seemed that whatever came to her mind, Jenny simply put it out there. While Jenny highly valued transparency, truth, and forthrightness, her lack of tact unfortunately cost her depth of relationship with her close friends, husband, and even her kids. She worked at rebuilding those relationships by reining in her lack of tact. Questions were one of her best tools.

People who have a tendency to blurt out whatever comes to mind without considering the effect on the recipient can benefit from reflecting on previous incidents where they expressed themselves disrespectfully, asking questions such as:

- "Are there kinder ways I could have said that?"
- "Was this the correct setting to make that statement?"
- "Were my comments age (or gender, race, faith) appropriate in this context?"

Based on Jenny's tragic relationship-wrecking experiences caused by her outspokenness, she formulated her own set of questions from a position of, "What questions do I wish somebody had asked me before I blurted out my opinion?" Jenny also alerted her friends about her desire to redirect her traditional approach and to soften her extremely blunt nature. She asked them to ask her questions to help her live within new boundaries and armed herself with a handful of questions to ask herself so she can think differently, such as:

- "Is it my place to say something here and now?"
- "Is there a better way I could say this?"
- "How might my comments be perceived?"
- "Can I ask this as a question instead of making a bold statement?"
- "Will it be best to keep my mouth shut altogether?"

Jenny is now well on her way to relearning a pattern of behavior that was causing injury and wounding relationships around her.

Using questions to create boundaries and guidelines helps us focus more quickly in conversations. "Can I ask you a question?" is too vague of a boundary, and it does not actually help. A more specific question such as, "Can I ask you about your shirt?" will narrow or set up a conversation. This helps your brain to begin looking for information. Mind mapping begins with focus and intentionality: "Is he going to ask where I bought it? Let me think. Where *did* I buy it?" as opposed to concern or wondering, "He wants to ask a question? About what? Did I make a mistake? Am I in trouble?" General questions can provoke our minds toward all kinds of possibilities, both good and bad. Focused boundaries of communication send our brain on a journey looking for specific memories and understandings.

Sherrie

On the other end of the boundary spectrum from Jenny is Sherrie. She rarely said "no." She was a classic doormat who allowed others to walk all over her by not speaking up. She said "yes" to virtually every request that came her way. Sherrie felt guilty when she was not doing more to help. She was likely the most overloaded employee in her workplace. Her boss thought of her as the go-to person when he did not know who else to ask. Sherrie would always find the time to add one more thing to her project list. We identified that her father had an extended season of unemployment in her teen years, so she had a fear of losing her job and would do everything within her power to ensure work stability.

Sherrie's kids only had to mildly complain to avoid any household chores because she felt it was her job to look after the house and was terrified to think that her kids would not like her if she asked them to help. Sherrie perceived her mother, who had worked to make ends meet, as a despised-by-her-kids "taskmaster" in years past. Sherrie lived in the fear of having her kids hate her.

Sherrie's husband routinely expected her to join him for dinner when he met new clients. He felt like he was a "conversational klutz" and that when Sherrie, the life of the party, was around, he always landed the clients. He sometimes asked that she host them for an elaborate meal. He moderately helped with those events, but regardless, it was twice the work for Sherrie compared to a regular meal.

As well, Sherrie refused to put her ailing mother in a nursing home. She felt overwhelming guilt if she did not visit her three or four times a week.

Sherrie was headed on a fast track towards burnout until she learned to ask herself these questions:

- "Why am I doing this?"
- "Can I say 'no'?"
- "What am I afraid of?"
- "Is that a rational fear?"
- "What are my options other than saying 'yes'?"
- "Can I say 'wait' or 'maybe' instead of 'no'?"
- "What is a reasonable boundary for this situation?"

Sherrie carried this short list of questions around with her in her purse and would quickly grab it when she felt pressured, bullied, or obligated. Her equilibrium came when her kids were expected to do a list of chores everyday if they wanted Internet privileges, even to do homework. Meanwhile her husband promised only one client meeting a month, and she committed to seeing her mom every Wednesday and Sunday, except for legitimate emergencies. Personal service workers who visited her Mom's home twice a week were on call to handle most problems. Sherrie's boss stopped pressuring her to take on extra projects since she said "no" to the last four requests. She has not received a raise or a promotion, but she had not received either when she was saying "yes" all the time. She still had her job with the same salary.

Sherrie had finally instituted all of these small boundaries to improve her life. Consequently, she felt less stress, the blotchy spots on her arms (which her doctor said were stress related) remarkably disappeared, she slept better, and she was much happier at work and home. For the first time in a decade she had time to visit with friends and take up hobbies. No longer held hostage by her ridiculously high expectations for herself, Sherrie could enjoy life much more now that she used her question list to help her establish boundaries.

Jordan

Jordan was another gentleman that really needed help with boundaries. He had a lovely wife, Jeanetta, who was 200 pounds overweight and depended on Jordan for everything. He had been an adventurous athlete all of his life. He played football, hiked, golfed, and wind-surfed before he met Jeanetta. In their early dating life, she shared with Jordan that she had been sexually assaulted as a 13-year-old, and that she felt very safe with him. They got engaged three months into their dating relationship. Jeanetta gained 50 pounds before they were married and another 150 pounds over the next four years. Jordan was out of shape, but had not put on any weight. He had adopted a sedentary lifestyle on evenings and weekends to keep his wife company watching TV and playing bridge with her and her bridge friends.

Jordan had some health issues from his earlier days that resurfaced with his less active lifestyle. When his doctor encouraged him to take up exercise again, Jeanetta pushed back, saying that she did not want to be alone and that her knees were "a mess" with all this weight she had gained. When Jordan had a mild heart attack at 39, he knew it was time to take back control of his life. He acknowledged that he and Jeanetta were codependent, and he started to own his own issues. One question really changed his life. As he would flounder in excuses about being out of shape, about Jeanetta - her past and her pain - he found health and healing by asking himself, "Is that my problem?"

That simple question helped Jordan disentangle himself from what were his own problems, and what were Jeanetta's problems. He decided to get healthy regardless of what Jeanetta decided, and he did get healthy. He started jogging, joined a health club, and a men's accountability group. He met all of his health targets in four months!

It took Jeanetta over a year to agree to come for counselling. By then, Jordan was in much better shape and well on the road to good health. Jeanetta, after another 10 months, still had a way to go, but she had lost almost a third of her target weight and worked through her crippling emotional scars. She took responsibility for her own pain that she had been hoping Jordan could fix. Jordan used to feel responsible for it. Now he is free from her secondhand emotional burdens. They are getting free from depending on each other and their marriage is moving towards health.

Kurt

Kurt was very likeable and personable. He had great stories and was highly intelligent. However, he got cynical on the days he was temperamental and moody, a result of unresolved anger. As he was passive-aggressive, he dealt with his anger through jokes and sarcasm. When he got upset, he rarely shared his frustration with anyone; rather, he mumbled as he walked away from a conversation. He did, however, moan and complain to his wife Leanne about issues at work from time to time.

Leanne has felt the brunt of Kurt's passive-aggressive nature. He would not say anything about a small issue for the longest time even though it ate him up inside. For example, about a year ago, he sulked as he listened to his wife complain about how she had lost one of her best friends when Kurt spontaneously left a couples' weekend getaway at a friend's cottage. During that weekend, Kurt had written off this couple because of some political contributions they had made to the party he did not agree with. When it came time for dinner, where the host had barbequed steaks for them, Leanne and Kurt had left without informing anyone. Understandably, the host was offended that they left without notice.

Leanne was not angry with anyone; Kurt was. However, with his inability to express his anger, Kurt was inadvertently hurting and even ending relationships.

Really, all he needed was to give the common courtesy of saying, "I'm leaving." Instead, he had become so angry that his judgment was clouded. He was too enmeshed in the desire to flee instead of fight. As he and Leanne debriefed later, he thought that if he had told them he was leaving he would have had to explain and resolve his differences, and he was not prepared to go there. It was easier for him to walk away giving no thought to the argument he may have avoided. Unfortunately, he gave no thought to the wasted steaks and the offense he created in bailing out on the planned dinner. Kurt, who had grown up in abusive foster homes, had not learned to talk through problems but rather to avoid them. He began to learn to talk through problems and apply boundaries.

The power of breakthrough questions

When individuals are defensive instead of open, there is a greater possibility of causing emotional and relational damage. As has been presented throughout this book, questions help to create understanding. Individuals in a relationship usually learn what topics to avoid so as not to evoke a negative response. However, to increase communication, you can formulate questions to use in place of potentially combative statements. By developing a progression of questions, you can resolve situations crippled by defensiveness, remove barriers, and break through to a new level of communication.

Different types of questions can be used to help individuals work through different types of defensiveness (DMs). The following are examples of areas where questions can help to bring understanding.

1. Realization (Awareness)

When Kurt did not realize he was in denial about his behavior, appropriate questions could be asked to create awareness to facilitate self-realization. This would move him from an initial confrontation with truth or reality to a place of seeing his part in it and truly acknowledging his feelings. For example:

- "How did the situation make you feel?"
- "Do you think you were feeling rejected?"
- "Do you think you might have felt hurt?"

2. Identification

Not only do questions confront and bring realization to a situation, they help identify or label what is going on. As discussed in chapter 7, when individuals feel insecure, they employ a defense mechanism (DM) to provide some form of emotional protection. When the threat is no longer present, the DM is no longer needed and therefore minimized or ignored. However, when the DM is not processed and resolved, the hurt feelings that were protected by the DM will remain dormant until triggered by a similar type experience. The old DM will reappear and will limit one's ability to honestly assess the behavior that needs to be changed so they can move on to a healthier, more emotionally relational place.

Do you remember the story of Brandon (chapter 7) and how he felt rejected by the girls in school? That feeling of rejection can persist for years. At some point, the DM(s) and underlying reason for the reaction needs to be resolved. Questions that can identify and process the emotional, relational health include:

- "Are you having difficulty accepting my concern for you?"
- "Do you think I don't care about you?"
- "Do you think that no one cares about you?"
- "Are you angry?"
- "Could your anger be blocking the care that I am trying to show you?"
- "Do you really want to act in a way that facilitates your feeling of rejection?"

3. Deterioration

Questions can expose the reality of a deteriorating situation. Exposure does not necessarily mean that it is condemning or judgmental; rather, it merely points out where the path could head if not corrected. Questions express an observation. For example:

- "Do you really want to spend the next year feeling sorry for yourself?"
- "Do you want to become an alcoholic?"
- "Do you want to keep hating people for the rest of your life?"
- "Do you like how this situation is going currently, how you feel currently?"
- "How is this situation working out for you?"
- "Do you want to keep feeling angry or hurt and acting out this way?"
- "Do you want to keep your friends at arm's length forever or can you talk this through?"

4. Solicitation

There is a proverb that essentially says that there is wisdom in getting wise counsel. Rather than assuming or feeling the pressure to come up with all the answers or to "fix it", you could solicit the help or knowledge of others. It is okay to ask for help. For example:

- "Can you help me?"
- "Can you help me to understand that?"
- "Who else could I talk to about this issue?"
- "Is there a friend, colleague, or peer I can trust with this struggle?"

- "Is there a coach, counsellor, priest, rabbi, or doctor I could make an appointment with?"
- "Am I comfortable talking to anyone about these serious issues and emotions?"

5. Transformation

True change of character and life transformation does not take place merely at a surface behavioral level. Changing a behavior is good, but when we help others understand their underlying motivations by asking questions, we enable them to identify both what they *want* to do with their life and *why*. As a result, we will have helped them to change at a deeper level. Questions that facilitate this level of change may include:

- "What goals do you have for yourself emotionally?"
- "Can you talk about what kind of person you want to be?"
- "Do you want to be able to freely be open and talk about negative emotions or
- things that bother you?"
- "How can you get to that point?"
- "Who can you surround yourself with to ensure forward progress?"

Perhaps at this point, asking deep questions may seem beyond the sphere of possibility for you. Learning how to ask questions is a lot like being in a swimming pool before you have learned how to swim. It is easy to stay in the shallow end or to wear floatation devices to feel safe. While it may be more comfortable to stay in the safe end of the pool, you cannot conquer the fear of the pool until you have learned how to swim. If you truly want to develop and overcome the fear of water, you must develop skills and practice swimming in the deep end. When you look back on those initial experiences of heading into the deep end, you might wonder what had been so frightening before.

In the same way, humans are designed to relate, and you can learn to ask questions. Although at first it is uncomfortable, the questions awkward, or the answers not quite what you were expecting, eventually you will venture out a little further into more challenging topics and questions. You will discover how questions build the bridge between the shallow topics and the deep subjects, slowly but surely. You do not have to be a counsellor to get to know people in a deeper way. Questions can enrich relationships with people in general and can enrich your life with a few deeply trusted friends.

Chapter 13

Practice, practice, practice

"For the things we have to learn before we
can do them, we learn by doing them."
– Aristotle

Intensity

If you are going to become a better communicator
and get better at relationship, you are going to have
to work at it with intensity. What does that mean?
Intensity is the physiological response to heightened
athletic competition. Intensity is a term used by sports
psychologists. It is contrasted by "anxiety" (a negative
term) and "energy" (a positive description). Positive
intensity happens when the heart rate is up, adrenaline
is increased, and all of the fight-or-flight neurological
responses are engaged. The effects of positive intensity
help when you are about to run, fight, or engage in any

271

strenuous physical activity. Negative intensity occurs when the body is engaged, ready to compete, but the more finely tuned motor skills are required. For example, the golfer does not want to be "all pumped up" and excited when teeing off as a high level of intensity could hurt their accuracy at this moment. Depending on the skill required in any given moment of competition, an athlete is not looking for over-intensity or under-intensity; rather, the quest is for optimal intensity.

When you engage in intense conversation, especially when emotion is high, you need a measure of preparation, understanding, and confidence that will optimally prepare you for such engagements. You can actually make yourself ready to participate in even the most uncomfortable circumstances imaginable. You can develop a skillset that will dramatically help with such encounters.

Scripting for change

I am certain that most of us want to be better communicators and better listeners. You can hope or wish to become a better communicator, but it is another thing to actually commit to changing the way you communicate. Joachim Grabowski has written about how you can impact your communication by writing things down; Grabowski calls it the "Writing Superiority Effect."[18] It is really quite simple when you break it down.

When you think about how you are going to communicate thoughts during a conversation, your mind kicks into gear to process what you are going to say. For example, when you think about things that you just heard the other participants in the conversation say, your participation is most likely to be spontaneous and superficial. Discourse protocol, however, goes a little deeper as you reflect on things you have heard, thought about, read, processed, or even written. It is good to hear it, better to read it, even better to re-read the information, and better yet to write the information down.

Dr. Caroline Leaf, whose material was utilized in chapter six, has developed Metacognitive Mapping, education strategies based on creating new neural pathways. In her book *Switch On Your Brain*, Dr. Leaf embraces increased academic and neurological development not based on memory work, but on *thinking* about thinking. Dr. Leaf attests, "If you teach a person to think deeply, they can do anything."[19] Traditional thought views the mind as a muscle: the more you work it, the stronger it gets. Other research suggests that rote memorization does little to improve your ability to *think*. Switching on your brain is more about metacognitive activities – *thinking* about thinking.

Leaf's Metacognitive Mapping is a process of writing down visual thinking into the leaves and branches of a mind-map. "Thinking to understanding" teaches individuals to think about what they are thinking about. Such thinking exercises train the mind to think deeper. As people analyze and understand what they are mapping, they reflect the deeper nerve networks and neural pathways that reflect what they are thinking about. It is an effective tool for deepening one's thought processes. Essentially, what we write as we prepare for a conversation does not need to follow specific sequential scripts; it could also follow diagrams which branch out like a map and follow the many possible routes of conversation. The focus of Leaf's perspective is to open our minds and to switch on our brains to learn how to think about our thoughts at a deeper level.

When you have time to prepare, write, or script a conversation, you are better prepared to converse. When you write down thoughts in advance, perhaps even several options of how you think a conversation might go, you are better prepared mentally as your mind has time to think through topics at a deeper level. Grabowski points out that we have more time per unit as we write our thoughts. He states that individuals normally speak at a rate of 160-180 words per minute (wpm), read at a rate of 200-250 wpm, and think at a rate of 500+ wpm. However, when it comes to writing, the normal range you can write is at a rate of 20-30 wpm. Just think of it. You think over 500 words in a minute but can only write 30 words in that minute. Consequently, the amount of time that you spend on each word and each thought is significantly higher when you read and write it, rather than just think it.

Grabowski also talks about pacing. Speaking, he says, requires a continued process; when writing, however, you can stop and ruminate for a time before you move on, an option you do not necessarily have when in conversation. Having a conversation is a good way to communicate, but Grabowski adamantly and convincingly develops the research-backed argument that writing out thoughts is a far superior way of communicating effectively.

However, it may not always be conducive to the conversation to excuse yourself saying, "Pardon me, I must excuse myself for a few minutes. I first need to manufacture a script of what I'm about to say next."

Imagine a married couple that has essentially been having the same argument several times or maybe avoiding the subject because they cannot find resolution. If they are truly committed to change, it makes sense for them to take the time to write out in advance what they want to say. This is why I frequently encourage my clients to script that difficult conversation, review it, and do it. Writing it out makes for better listeners, communicators, and thinkers.

Practice

"It's not God-given. It's Wally-given." – Wayne Gretzky

Wayne Gretsky, probably the greatest hockey player ever, suggests that his hockey skill isn't so much a God-given talent as it is something that his father Wally built into him. Wayne spent many cold winter nights skating around bleach bottles on his family's backyard rink to practice his skills. He also shot countless pucks at a piece of plywood on that same rink, learning to perfect his shot. Gretzky was not the biggest, strongest, or fastest player, but he incessantly practiced anticipating where the puck was going to be, not where it had just been.

"Practice makes perfect" is more than just an old cliché. There are actual scientific studies that support this statement. Functional magnetic resonance imaging (fMRI) brain scans reveal heightened brain activity that increases during learning, but as the activity or function becomes natural or instinctive (like driving a car with a manual transmission) the brain activity lessens as the task has been learned and mastered. The more we practice, the less we think, thus enabling us to focus on variables and finer points of function that allow us to perfect any task we repeatedly engage in.

The phrase "practice makes perfect" applies to the area of communication as well. By mentally going over a conversation or scripting it in advance, you will improve your overall communication skillset.

Sample Scripts

The following three scripts are examples that can help you to develop your own scripts for the issues relevant to your relationship. You can create your own questions or use ones from the examples. You will find that as you practice and implement the questions in face-to-face conversations, you will create your own style of questions and questioning. Give yourself permission to not be perfect when you first use questions in communication. You will get better at it.

1. Couples

a. Scenario 1

Peter and Sheila have fights whenever his parents visit. His parents have difficulty respecting boundaries. Usually, before Peter's parents leave, Sheila wants to leave. Conflict about their disrespect becomes a sore spot in their relationship for weeks afterward. Sheila is nervous about talking to her husband regarding the issue, but she believes it is better to deal with the problem before it escalates each time the parents visit. She plans to have the conversation Tuesday night when Peter is home for the evening. A favorite snack and drink will be ready for Peter to create an optimal mood for good conversation and to minimize Peter's defensiveness when talking about his parents. Sheila envisions the script happening as follows:

> Sheila: "I'm glad the kids are all sleeping. Can we talk now for 10 or 15 minutes about your parents coming this weekend? It's not about you Peter. It's just about planning to make sure it goes well."
> Peter: "Sure, I'm listening."
> Sheila: "I know you have been a bit dismissive about this subject in the past, but this
> issue is important to me. I have found their last few visits have been personally hurtful, so could you just hear me out on this?"
> Peter: "Yeah, fair enough. An ounce of prevention is worth a pound of cure, right? This makes sense to talk about in advance. You have my attention."
> Sheila: "I promise to be short so we can still relax tonight and have some free time. You can enjoy your snack as we chat. Is that okay?"
> Peter: "Okay. But I won't hold you to your statement about it being a short conversation."
> Sheila: "Yeah. Thanks, Honey. I need your help with a few boundaries. Can you help me?"
> Peter: "If I can help, I will."
> Sheila: "It's your dad and mom and I don't want to be disrespectful, especially to them, or you for that matter."
> Peter: "I'm not sure what kind of boundaries you need."

Sheila: "First, do you know that I know you're on my side?"

Peter: "Yes I do."

Sheila: "Also, do you know that I know that I can't do this alone and I really, really need your help?"

Peter: "And I do want to help."

Sheila: "What boundaries could we set?"

Peter: "I'm not quite sure that I know what the issues are."

Sheila: "Can I tell you?"

Peter: "Go ahead."

Sheila: "Well, the first thing that comes to mind is that your dad can be rough and curt as you know. He tends to pick on me for being a housewife, like that's not good enough. He still thinks I should have a job even though we have three kids under the age of five. Do you think I should be working?"

Pete: "Definitely not! We've talked about this several times. What can I do to help you?"

Sheila: "Well, if you hear him going down this road, can you please just set a boundary for him by letting him know that this is your decision too and that you value me being a stay-at-home mom? And my job is important even though I don't get paid?"

Peter: "Yeah. That's a good idea. I've got your back on this. What else?"

Sheila: "If he makes any sexual jokes or innuendos or anything like that, you know I'm uncomfortable talking or joking about that stuff with them, right?"

Peter: "Yeah. If he goes there at all in front of me, I will shut it down."

Sheila: "Can you also promise me that you won't get into it along with him?"

Peter: "Right. Yeah, I have done that before. He gets me laughing sometimes. I will try to keep it more serious. Sorry. I will remember this time. Anything else?"

Sheila: "Yep. In a minute. But let me say first, it's okay if your dad pulls you in with a joke. He's spontaneous and witty, but just don't let him carry on like he does or turn raunchy. That's the part that gets me. You can still have fun, but just don't let him go too far or cross a line. Does that make sense?"

Peter: "Totally. I'm good with that."

Sheila: "The other thing. I know your mom is usually pretty good and we get along very well, but sometimes she does this guilt thing when I make a comment like 'I'm glad you're here,' or 'It's good to see you' and she'll snap at me like, 'Well, if we don't come here we'd never see the grandkids' or 'You haven't been to visit us since Christmas.' Doesn't she remember what it's like to have kids? Does she remember what it was

like to travel in a car for two hours with kids? How do we curb those kinds of comments?"
Peter: "How about this? If she pulls one of her closet guilt trips, why don't you just walk away and ask me out loud 'Hey Peter, do you know what your mom just asked me?' and start telling me as you walk towards me, even if I'm in the basement. Come find me. That will keep her accountable to not sneak behind my back. Dad will be ticked off too if she pulls that guilt stuff. He hates that. If we let her get away with it unchecked, the guilt trips will only get worse. Trust me. I know after 20 years under her roof."
Sheila: "Thanks for having my back."

Rather than the parental visits being a continual source of irritation and conflict for Peter and Sheila, Sheila has taken it upon herself to troubleshoot before the visit this time. It is good for Sheila to proactively address the conflict issues well in advance and to talk about possible action steps and trust Peter to be on her side. By reaffirming his love and support for her, she feels comfortable reminding Peter of the boundaries he committed to when they married, even if he is still somewhat ignorant of his parents' manipulations.

b. Scenario 2

Jack and Shelly have only been married three years, but Jack is really upset with Shelly. He has confronted her several times about spending beyond their agreed-upon budget. As Jack has scripted out some of their prior conversations, he has come to some significant revelations concerning the budget as he writes and reviews what he has written:

> Jack: "I must confess. Picking you up at work today for a quick lunch is not just about being romantic and spontaneous. I also needed to talk to you about an important matter. I'm very committed to you and I love you and I wanted to take 15 minutes of our lunch hour to talk about budgeting and also to own my part in that conflict."
>
> Shelly: "What? So, I can spend whatever I want to spend now? Are you going to point out all of my indiscretions now on the credit card statement? I don't believe this. You always do this. You treat me nice and then hit me with some heavy thing like our finances. I'm not ready for an ambush today on my lunch hour."
>
> Jack: "I always do this? Did I do this last Thursday night when we went for a walk?"
>
> Shelly: (Silent)
>
> Jack: "Did I do this last month when I brought you sushi at work when you didn't have time for a lunch break that day? And did I bring up something negative when I took you for a latté and then to see the sunrise on the way to dropping you off early at your breakfast meeting?"

Shelly: (Still silent, arms folded, brow furrowed)

Jack: "And didn't we agree last month at the couples' group therapy that stonewalling was out of bounds in our discussions? Silence is unacceptable. We agreed on that right?"

Shelly: "Yeah. Sorry. I'm just upset and hate talking about finances."

Jack: "Do you think that I enjoy the tension that talking about the finances causes?"

Shelly: "No. I don't believe that you bring the topic up just to cause tension in our relationship."

Jack: "Do you think that I like feeling shut out when I want to talk about something that is important to me and ultimately to us?"

Shelly: "No. I get it. I just don't like the topic because it feels like I am going to be told off and then controlled with respect to my spending. That scares me and causes me to become defensive."

Jack: "Well, I do want to apologize if my issues make you feel afraid and defensive. I'll address that in a minute. Can we at least agree on a couple things?"

Shelly: "Like what?"

Jack: "That we can't just spend whatever we want, whenever we want?"

Shelly: "Sure."

Jack: "That there still have to be reasonable, mutually agreed upon boundaries around our finances?"

Shelly: "Possibly. I'm not sure what boundaries you are thinking about, but I do agree that there should be some kind of boundaries."

Jack: "Regarding my apology. I know that I created a lot of stress with my three-year plan to save up for a deposit on a house, get out of the apartment, get settled, fix up the place, and have kids by year five of our marriage. I've been way too strict to make the plan work by year three. But then I also remembered that I was the one who wanted to do it in three years. You had initially suggested four or five years. Saving up for the deposit in three years was nuts! What was I thinking? The budget is way too tight. So, I'm sorry for that. I was probably too pushy on that issue. Can you please forgive me for that?"

Shelly: "Yeah. Thanks. You are forgiven. It has been tight. It was too quick. I'm frustrated with how tight things are. Our emergency cushion money is all gone. I hate living like this."

Jack: "What do you think is a plan that you would be able to work with?"

Shelly: "I think if we work on getting into a house within five years that I could live with spending a little less to make that happen."

Jack: "Okay. Agreed. I will re-work the budget to reflect a savings plan that could be done over five years. When *do* you want to have kids? What are your thoughts? Should we change the plan?"

Shelly: "I don't know. I don't think I'm ready for a baby in two years. Maybe not even three or four more years. Yeah, we probably should alter the timeline."

Jack: "Well, if that's the case, do you want to put off buying a house for another two years rather than driving towards our artificially imposed deadline for the fall of this year? Who says we have to stick to that?"

Shelly: "Well, I don't think so. I really do want to get into our own house ASAP."

Jack: "Yeah? Are you sure? How about we just put it off one year and not two?"

Shelly: "I could live with that."

Jack: "Even at one year, we would still have to make some sacrifices financially. Are you ready for that?"

Shelly: "I think so."

Jack: "What would you be willing to sacrifice to make our home purchase a reality in 18 months? No vacations? No new outfits? No new furniture?"

Shelly: "I want a vacation more than I want clothes or other stuff. How about we do one really nice vacation this summer, like a cruise, and then I could be prepared to sacrifice for the next 13 or 14 months to meet our savings goals? And our first year in the house, maybe we'll stick with the plan to spend vacation time working on renovations? I love doing that stuff."

Jack: "I could easily concede that. It sounds good to me. Are you comfortable with that?"

Shelly: "Yeah. I feel good about that. So, Mr. Big Spender, are you taking me to the Ritz for lunch?"

Jack: "I was actually thinking of somewhere to get a burger."

Shelly: "Wow. If we put off buying the house for another year, can I get fries with that?"

2. Work

Scenario

Matt Scott has been Jeff's boss for three years at a local company. Jeff wants to ask for a raise since he is about to get married.

Jeff: "Thank you for taking this appointment with me, Mr. Scott. Did your assistant mention what the appointment was about?"

Matt: "Yes, Jeff, she did mention that you wanted to discuss your current salary. And please, call me Matt. So, tell me, what are your thoughts regarding increasing your salary?"

Jeff: "I want you to know that I truly appreciate this job. Thank you for hiring me years ago and for seeing potential in me and believing in me. I believe that I have been a very good employee here, I have brought in dozens of new clients, and have sold over $2 million worth of product in the last three years. Knowing what our profit margin is, even after my salary and expenses are paid, I have still made this company over $500,000 of profit. I am grateful for my salary and I am grateful for how I am treated here. However, I would like to request a raise.

Matt: "Jeff, your HR file says that although you are on time, you tend to loiter in the lunch room, fraternize with other employees at the front desk, and play practical jokes on your co-workers, especially Doug. Can you explain this behavior for me?"

Jeff: "I'm glad you asked about that, that's a great question. As you know, our company has a corporate culture of caring about our employees, their families, and valuing healthy working relationships. I was merely trying to mirror the corporate culture. I have been initiating conversation with the receptionist and several of my co-workers so that, hopefully, we can function out of a relational paradigm rather than just have a cold, sterile office environment. My sales numbers are good and my performance is not hurting. I am just trying to be a good team player. Isn't that what is intended in our corporate culture documents? Have I interpreted that incorrectly?"

Matt: "No, that's a good interpretation. We want to work as teams, as friends, not strangers. However, our employee handbook discourages co-workers from dating. Aren't you getting married to the office manager?"

Jeff: "I am. However, the handbook discourages dating, but it does not forbid it."

Matt: "I'm happy for you, I really am. I don't want to hold you back in your career. I am open to talking more about giving you a raise. Maybe we could discuss it later this evening over dinner?"

Jeff: "I appreciate the invitation, but I don't think I'm comfortable meeting outside of office hours to talk about something as serious as this. I do have a family commitment this evening that I cannot break as well. I did book in one hour for this appointment. Can we just finish the conversation now?"

Matt: "Alright. Can you please tell me more about the details of your engagement?"

Jeff: "I'm sorry, but how is that relevant to our discussion?"

Matt: "No, you're right. It's not. Did I mention that the company is in a salary freeze right now? I don't think we can give you a raise."

Jeff: "Dwight just got a raise yesterday."

Matt: "Did he? Wow. That must have been an exception to that rule for some reason."

Jeff: "...and Toby said he was getting a raise at the end of this month!"

Matt: "Really? Wow. Okay. So, what's your point?"

Jeff: "I am by far your most productive employee. Other employees are getting a raise and I would like a raise as well."

Matt: "Can we meet next week sometime to discuss this further?"

Jeff: "Can you help me understand how come it is not possible to resolve this issue today?"

Matt: "I guess there's no reason. We still have some time."

Jeff: "Thank you."

Matt: "Okay. So how much were you anticipating for a raise?"

When you script out a conversation, you can deal with awkward topics and even awkward people. It will benefit you greatly to think ahead about what could possibly go wrong or how the conversation could be sidetracked. In such cases, we can prepare appropriate responses based on the history of conversations with that person. You can also anticipate emotional outbursts, defense mechanisms that might be used, or other potential pitfalls. It is one thing to read about how questions and other skills can help us with communication, but it is next level thinking and acting to prepare and practice with scripts.

Closing thoughts

Many of the concepts articulated in earlier chapters are reflected in the scripts. I encourage you to write your own scripts that would reflect the principles and ideas that stood out most to you. Remember: practice makes perfect. You can easily implement whatever is most needed and what works best for you. Often, unresolved conflicts remain unresolved when you do not take the time to script a conversation.

When there is a conflict, the negative feelings associated with the conflict are remembered most and, therefore, are most likely to be avoided when the conflict arises again and again. When you script out the conflict in a conversation, you can process the topic at a level that is more cognitive and less emotional. When you process at the cognitive level, it is more logical and rational, and therefore more likely to be more reasonable when implemented.

As previously stated, the more you practice scripting either on paper or in your mind, the less likely you are to get distracted by the feelings that are most commonly associated with the intensity the original conflict created. By practicing, you can anticipate what you are going to say, become more focused on the topic, and be less distracted by the emotions your partner may be expressing.

Distractions such as changing the topic, blaming, and increased emotional intensity are often just that: a distraction. When you know what you want to say, the direction you want to take the conversation, and how you want to say it by utilizing questions, as has been laid out in the previous chapters, you have a method and a direction. The more you apply this approach, the more confident you will become in being able to tackle difficult topics of conversation under difficult circumstances because the defense mechanism will be less likely to be used by either person in the conversation.

I believe that if you take the necessary steps to practice and implement these concepts, your communication will change, and your life and your relationships can be transformed. Give it a good effort. Don't quit or give up. It has worked for others. It can work for you.

CLOSING REFLECTIONS

While my wife and I were in the middle of renovations, we were on our way to look at flooring materials. On the drive, my wife commented about a product and design she had in mind. She expressed her opinion as to why she thought it was the best option.

"Do you agree?" she asked.

I listened and thought about how I did not feel the same way. I engaged my wife by responding to her question, telling her what I was thinking.

"I don't agree," I answered.

My response prompted my wife to further explain her reasoning and why I should see it from her perspective. I told her I did not see it that way and, therefore, could not agree with her opinion. She continued to delineate her opinion with great points, but I still could not agree.

After a couple rounds of discussion, I asked, "Can we agree to disagree?"

Unlike past experiences where we might have argued at length, she agreed to this, but added she had one more point to make with respect to why she believed her ideas were better than mine (after all, she is the decorator). "Sure," I responded, "but do you know that I may disagree with your point again?"

My wife said that she understood and then proceeded to make her last point. I listened, then stated that I still did not see it from her perspective. We carried on checking out the construction material and designs without disruption or tension. Eventually, we found something we could both agree on.

Maybe you see yourself in my story mentioned above. Or, maybe you see yourself in one of the scenarios described in this book. Well, you are not alone. Learning to listen means learning how to ask questions. Whether you develop this skill through engaging in personal or relationship counselling, or through asking questions to family members, friends, or work colleagues, you will find yourself more engaged and less frustrated. Further, you will be more accepting of others' perspectives and less likely to feel the need to have others agree with your perspective as you will be more focused on being understood.

The individuals you engage with your questions will either agree or disagree with you. Regardless of how convincing you might be, they may still disagree. Asking questions to gain understanding will save you time and emotional energy.

It may also save a relationship.

ENDNOTE

i   Gordon W. Allport." BrainyQuote.com, 2015.

ii   Jonah Lehrer, *The Decisive Moment: How the Brain Makes up its Mind*, Canongate Books, 2010, pg. 106

iii   *Marcus Aurelius Meditations*, Book 8, Dent, 1961.

iv   Hansen, R. D.; Hansen, C. H. "Repression of emotionally tagged memories: The architecture of less complex emotions," *Journal of Personality and Social Psychology*, 55(5), 1988, pg. 811–818.

v   Bretherick, Graham, *The Fear Shift: Dominated by Fear No More*, Run Free Ministries, 2014, pg. 51

vi   Irene Goldenberg, *Family Therapy: An Overview*, Wadsworth Publishing Co Inc., 1985.

vii   Bretherick, Graham, *The Fear Shift: Dominated by Fear No More*, Run Free Ministries, 2014.

viii Andrew Newberg M.D. and Mark Robert Waldman, *How God Changes Your Brain: Breakthrough Findings from a Leading Neuroscientist*, Ballantine Books, 2010, pg. 19.

ix Andrew Newberg M.D. and Mark Robert Waldman, *How God Changes Your Brain: Breakthrough Findings from a Leading Neuroscientist*, Ballantine Books, 2010, pg. 20.

x Dr. John M. Gottman, *The Seven Principles for Making Marriage Work: A Practical Guide from the Country's Foremost Relationship Expert*, Harmony Books, 2000.

xi Gottman Method Couples Therapy Level 1 Clinical Training, The Gottman Institute, Section 1, pg. 2.

xii Erwin Raphael McManus, *The Artisan Soul: Crafting Your Life into a Work of Art*, Harperone, 2014

xiii Alison King, "Inquiring Minds Really Do Want to Know: Using Questioning to Teach Critical Thinking," *Teaching of Psychology* 22, 1995, pg. 14.

xiv Karima Merchant, "How Men And Women Differ: Gender Differences in Communication Styles, Influence Tactics, and Leadership Styles," Open Access Senior Thesis, Claremont McKenna College, 2012.

xv John Gray, *Men Are from Mars, Women Are from Venus: The Classic Guide to Understanding the Opposite Sex*, Harper Paperbacks, 1992.

xvi   Deborah Tannen, *You Just Don't Understand: Women and Men in Conversation*, William Morrow Paperbacks, 2013.

xvii   John Townsend, *Boundaries: When to Say Yes, How to Say No to Take Control of Your Life*, Zondervan, 1992.

xviii Joachim Grabowski, "The Writing Superiority Effect in the Verbal Recall of Knowledge: Sources and Determinants," *Studies in Writing*, 2007.

xix   Dr. Caroline Leaf, *Switch On Your Brain: The Key to Peak Happiness, Thinking, and* Health, Baker Books, 2013.